I WAS UNDER A HEAVY BURDEN

Funding for this book was given in honor of
Dr. Ervin Seamster

I WAS UNDER A HEAVY BURDEN

THE LIFE OF ANNIE C. TUGGLE

EDWARD J. ROBINSON

Abilene Christian University Press

I WAS UNDER A HEAVY BURDEN

The Life of Annie C. Tuggle

ACU PRESS

ISBN 978-0-89112-548-8
LCCN 2011022890

Printed in the United States of America

Scripture quotations noted KJV are taken from the King James Version of the Bible.

LIBRARY OF CONGRESS CATALOGING-IN-PUBLICATION DATA
Robinson, Edward J., 1967-
I was under a heavy burden : the life of Annie C. Tuggle / Edward J. Robinson.
p. cm.
Includes bibliographical references and index.
ISBN 978-0-89112-548-8 (alk. paper)
1. Tuggle, Annie C., 1890-1976. 2. Churches of Christ--Biography. 3. African American women--Religious life. 4. African Americans--Religion. 5. United States--Church history--20th century. I. Title. II. Title: Life of Annie C. Tuggle.
BX7077.Z8T84 2011
286.6092--dc23
[B]

2011022890

Cover photo courtesy of Laura J. Dawson.
Photos used for Part II and III courtesy of Bernice M. Pitts.

Cover design by Rick Gibson
Interior text design by Sandy Armstrong

For information contact:
Abilene Christian University Press
1626 Campus Court
Abilene, Texas 79601

1-877-816-4455
www.abilenechristianuniversitypress.com

11 12 13 14 15 16 / 7 6 5 4 3 2 1

To
Patricia Evans
and
Bernice Pitts,
faithful soldiers of the cross.

And to
the memory of
Michael W. Casey
(1954-2007)
and
Earl I. West
(1920-2011),
exemplary scholars and encouraging mentors.

CONTENTS

PROLOGUE

"UNDER A HEAVY BURDEN"

W. E. B. Du Bois once offered a penetrating assessment of African American women in the early twentieth century: "As I look about me today in this veiled world of mine, despite the noisier and more spectacular advance of my brothers, I instinctively feel and know that it is the five million of my race who really count. Black women (and women whose grandmothers were black) are today furnishing our teachers; they are the main pillars of those social settlements which we call churches; and they have with small doubt raised three-fourths of our church property."[1] Du Bois's paean to African American women as concerned educators, economic supporters, and stabilizing forces in the African American community captures the essence of Annie Clay Tuggle, a singular black woman and a passionate and determined adherent of the Stone-Campbell religious reform movement.[2] Researchers of the African American experience in the Stone-Campbell Restoration Movement ordinarily have studied pivotal black preachers such as Marshall Keeble, G. P. Bowser, and R. N. Hogan,[3] but regrettably have ignored the invaluable contribution of such "main pillars" as Annie C. Tuggle.

After converting from Methodism to Churches of Christ in the early twentieth century, Tuggle soon emerged as a young woman of influence in a white- and male-dominated religious construct. When W. C. Baldwin, a young ministerial student from the Silver Point Christian Institute near Nashville, preached in Lancaster, Tennessee, an inquisitive young listener stood and asked: "What is wrong with the Methodist church?" Unable to answer the young lady's question, the inexperienced preacher called on Tuggle who possessed more biblical knowledge than he. Tuggle, revealing her exclusivistic theology, declared that since the "Methodist church and its doctrine" were not found in the Bible, they were not approved by God. Distraught that she had spoken out during the worship service, contravening the common practices of her church, Tuggle later confessed that "I was under a heavy burden because I had spoken in the midst of the congregation."[4] But throughout her life, the society of her native land imposed far more onerous burdens on Tuggle.

Like other contemporary black women in segregated America, Tuggle bore the double burdens of race and gender. Several scholars have carefully and poignantly assessed the plight of African American women during the eras of both chattel enslavement and de jure segregation. Historian Deborah Gray White has explored the "double oppression" enslaved black women encountered in the antebellum period,[5] and Jacqueline Jones has aptly noted that African American women bore a "doubly disadvantaged status" because of the racism and the sexism they continually faced.[6] Cynthia Neverdon-Morton, focusing on African American women in the post-Reconstruction South, concludes that black women shouldered the "double burden of race and sex,"[7] while Cynthia Griggs Fleming trenchantly captured the enduring struggle of African American women, asserting, "Being an oppressed *black* woman has always been quite different from being an oppressed woman in American society."[8]

Even though Annie C. Tuggle's life reflects the foregoing assessments of dual burdens of race and sex, it further reveals a suffusing spiritual subtext which fomented a complex layering to her personality. This study posits that Tuggle, an African American womanist[9] in a Restorationist fellowship, bore a trio of burdens—race, gender, and religion. White people devalued her because of her race, black men distrusted her because of her gender, and many outside of Churches of Christ spurned Tuggle because of her sectarian stance.[10] Tuggle's struggles attest that African American women were in no way monolithic. Despite her recurring frustration when facing the obstacles of racism, sexism, and religious intolerance, Tuggle left an indelible mark on the history of African American Churches of Christ.

Ironies and paradoxes marked Tuggle's eventful life. Her race barred her from most white Churches of Christ, yet she published several articles in the influential white-controlled, Nashville-based, *Gospel Advocate*.[11] Her chosen religious fellowship prohibited her from delivering public sermons due to her gender, yet she evangelized and organized an all-female church in West Tennessee. Tuggle, as a woman, could not occupy official leadership roles in Churches of Christ, yet she led Bible classes for women, read scripture for preachers in public gatherings, gave spiritual advice and direction to both white and black church leaders, answered biblical questions raised by diffident preachers, and became the first noteworthy chronicler of the history of African American Churches of Christ. Yet her zeal and sectarianism often repelled the very black people she desired to uplift.

Samuel Robert Cassius, a Tuggle contemporary, lamented the contradictory burden African Americans in Churches of Christ bore, regretting that "I have had to win my way through religious prejudice in my own race, and race prejudice among the brethren of my own faith."[12] Black believers in denominational churches rejected Cassius because they found his exclusivistic theology repugnant, and many whites in his own fellowship despised his race. Marshall Keeble, an admirer and mentor of Tuggle, testified more bluntly, "The white man didn't like me because of the color of my skin. The colored man didn't like me because of my religion."[13] This was the heavy and complex religious burden[14] that Tuggle shouldered in addition to the weighty loads of racism and sexism.

An analysis of Annie C. Tuggle, then, brings a unique voice to the black female conversation in the United States just as it adds to the richness and complexity of our view of black Christian women. Tuggle symbolizes the countless ordinary African American women who labored to help their people find their way within a distinctive religious construct situated in a viciously anti-black society with iron mandates enforced by implacable lynch law. A study of Tuggle's life, however, incurs severe difficulties and limitations since she left behind no collection of papers, nor did her religious fellowship create any extra-congregational bodies that might have preserved archives. A full length biographical study is, therefore, virtually impossible. But, Tuggle did bequeath to posterity her 1973 autobiography, *Another World Wonder,* a number of articles in the *Gospel Advocate,* a journal established by Tolbert Fanning and Lipscomb in 1855, and articles in the *Christian Echo,* a paper established by P. Bowser in 1902. Furthermore, several people in African American Churches of Christ, whose lives were touched and inspired by Tuggle, are still living, and their testimonies provide supplementary information and documentation, enriching this study.

I Was Under a Heavy Burden, appropriating a combination of chronological and thematic approaches, consists of six chapters in three parts. Chapter one delineates Tuggle's early life and family background, giving specific attention to the people and events that molded and shaped her character as a child and adolescent. It contends that Tuggle's mother had the most profound and enduring impact on her life as a moral guide and spiritual counselor. Chapter two traces Tuggle's spiritual journey from Methodism to Churches of Christ as well as her academic pilgrimage from Lane College in Jackson, Tennessee, to LeMoyne Normal Institute in Memphis, and eventually to her place as a thirty-three-year-old valedictorian of Walden College in Tennessee's capital city.

While chapter three examines the sexism and other personal struggles Tuggle encountered in both society and the church, chapter four explores the paradox that Tuggle, although a childless woman, still exerted profound influence on many black youths in Churches of Christ chiefly through the agency of the Nashville Christian Institute where she taught. So even though Tuggle never birthed children of her own, she spiritually mothered many young black people. Chapter five then probes Tuggle's militant use of the Bible, comparing and contrasting her view of scripture with those of her male and female counterparts within and without Churches of Christ. Finally, chapter six assesses Tuggle's autobiography in its literary and historical contexts, giving special attention to her labor as a historian in Southern California, where she died in 1976.

Precocious, assertive, and deeply committed to God, Tuggle devoted her life to the "salvation and education"[15] of black Americans in a racially oppressive milieu. Like all African Americans, she struggled to define her "place" in a virulently racist society, a rigidly sexist environment, and a theologically exclusivistic fellowship. Largely because of her Restorationist affinity and myopic theological perspectives, Tuggle did not gain the renown earned by such black paladins as Sojourner Truth, Harriet Jacobs, Harriet Tubman, Ida B. Wells, Fannie Lou Hamer, or Rosa Parks. Notwithstanding her historical invisibility in popular culture, Tuggle's story is both noteworthy and praiseworthy because, in the words of historian Evelyn Brooks Higginbotham, she helped make the African American church the "most powerful institution of racial self-help in the African American community."[16] Her life further elucidates the observation of Deborah Gray White that African American women were never a "monolithic group" nor a "harmonious sisterhood,"[17] and validates the contention of Cheryl Gilkes that *If It Wasn't for the Women,* there would not be a black church.[18] The tale of Annie C. Tuggle not only represents the complex intersecting of race, gender, and religion, but also enriches and enhances our understanding of the African American religious experience particularly and the American past generally.

PART I

THE BURDEN OF RACE

1890–1923

Annie C. Tuggle

CHAPTER 1

"A DEBT OF GRATITUDE THAT CAN NEVER BE PAID"

The Early Life

"The ruler of home is mother. A faithful, virtuous and intelligent motherhood will elevate any people. The impress of mother follows her children to the grave; when her form is changed and her physical existence extinct the footprints of her noble and pious life will live long after her."[1]

—Sarah Dudley Pettey (ca. 1870s)

Racial violence, economic disparity, social upheaval, and international conflict shaped the last decade of the nineteenth century. Between 1890 and 1892, rampaging white mobs lynched an astonishing 380 African Americans across the New South. In the spring of 1892, an enraged and envious mob in Memphis, Tennessee, brutally murdered Tom Moss, Calvin McDowell, and Lee Stewart, three black grocer competitors and close friends of

Ida B. Wells. Before his savage execution, Moss pled piteously with his family and other black Memphians to "go West" because "there is no justice for them here." The heinous murder inspired Wells to launch an international anti-lynching campaign, and it underscored the tragic reality that African Americans across the land "lived under the shadow of fear and violence."[2] And in 1896 the United States Supreme Court codified the "separate but equal" doctrine in *Plessy v. Ferguson*, in essence stripping African Americans of civil rights hardly won during the Reconstruction era.[3]

Beyond the racial hostility dogging black southerners, all Americans felt the pangs of economic hardship in the 1890s. The Panic of 1893 drove struggling families to draw down on their meager savings, to send their children to live with more prosperous neighbors, and to scour city streets in search of coal, wood, and food. Jacob Coxey led a host of disgruntled and destitute farmers on the nation's capital in 1894 to demand jobs and monetary relief.[4] The grinding economic problems aroused frustrated farmers to league with the rising Populist Party which agitated for political, financial, agricultural, and transportation reform.[5] In 1898 the Spanish–American War, "a splendid little war" saturated with racist overtones, led to the acquisition of Cuba, Guam, Puerto Rico, and the Philippines, establishing the United States as an emerging world power.[6] In this milieu, one poet urged white Americans to "take up the White Man's burden" of disseminating supposed superior white culture to so-called inferior brown and black peoples at home and abroad.[7] In this tumultuous decade emerged a little black girl from West Tennessee, Annie C. Tuggle, who would eventually bear multiple burdens to make life better for black people in the United States.

Even though much of Annie C. Tuggle's early life remains clouded, her autobiography, *Another World Wonder*, offers some illumination of her formative years. Her paternal grandfather, Charles Tuggle, was a native of Hagerstown, Maryland, one of 90,368 enslaved Africans in the state during the mid-nineteenth century.[8] Even though chattel enslavement in the Upper South was reputed to be more mild and humane,[9] Frederick Douglass, an enslaved African from Talbot County, Maryland, knew first-hand the arduous labor and horrid living conditions, and he witnessed merciless beatings and the "pain of separation" that enslaved Africans suffered in his native state.[10] Like many enslaved Africans in the antebellum South, Charles Tuggle experienced the profoundly excruciating pain of ruthless family destruction at the age of thirteen when he and his mother were sold and transported to New Orleans, Louisiana. From there his mother was mercilessly sold and transported to East Texas, while her young son Charles was purchased by Phillip Tuggle, a prosperous landowner and Methodist preacher from Shelby County, Tennessee.[11]

Slaveowners in Tennessee, unlike their Maryland counterparts, tended to be more numerous and more affluent.[12] At the eve of the Civil War, Phillip Tuggle reportedly owned ten thousand dollars in real estate and had a total net worth of twenty thousand dollars.[13] Phillip, his wife, Mary, and their three children, Joseph, Phillip Jr., and Anna, devoutly followed the Methodist faith.[14] Charles Tuggle, one of Phillip Sr.'s thirty-four slaves,[15] embraced Methodism and transmitted it to his family. Because of his diligence and "faithful service" as a farmer and janitor at the Methodist Church on Phillip Tuggle's property, Charles received monetary compensation which he frugally managed. By emancipation he had accumulated five hundred dollars and had married Louisa Wills, with whom he had five children: Townsend, Haywood, Sophia, Addie, and Emma.[16]

While several scholars have documented African Americans' attraction to Methodism because of its freshness, simplicity, and emotionalism,[17] it appears that Annie's grandfather was won over to the Methodist faith because of the cordial treatment by its white members as well as the opportunity to advance materially. Indeed, by 1880 Charles had committed himself to the preaching ministry of the Colored Methodist Episcopal (CME) Church and had acquired three hundred acres of land in Germantown, Tennessee, plentiful livestock, and black servants who "ate daily at his table," making him one of the more than 400,000 black landowners after emancipation. His comfortable and commodious dwelling often welcomed CME Church dignitaries, including Bishop Isaac Lane.[18] Annie C. Tuggle and her family drew their material prosperity and their spiritual heritage from their diligent paternal grandfather, Charles Tuggle.

If religion and affluence shaped Annie's paternal heritage, miscegenation marked her maternal ancestry. Schuyler H. Roberts, the owner of twenty-seven slaves on a one thousand–acre farm in Shelby County, fathered Annie's maternal grandfather, Quinton Roberts, with one of his slaves, Mahalia.[19] Altogether Schuyler sired five children with Mahalia, and they "lived happily together until S. H. lawfully married a white mistress." The uniting of S. H. to a white woman stirred up "trouble" and prompted him to purchase a plantation in Paris, Tennessee, where he relocated Mahalia and their five children.[20]

Mr. Roberts's carnal relation with Mahalia and the ensuing hostility with his white wife reveal the complexity and turmoil that ensnared bi-racial families in the antebellum South. Solomon Northup, a free black man from New York who was captured and enslaved for twelve years in the South, reported that Louisiana slaveholder Edwin Epps's constant cohabitating with his slave, Patsey, kindled the ire of his wife. Mrs. Epps's rage "boiled at the sight of Patsey, and nothing less than trampling out the life of the helpless bondwoman would satisfy her."[21] While many white slave owners were, in the words of one scholar, "notorious in the neighborhood"[22] and frequently raped their black female slaves, some few genuinely loved and cared for their black women and their mixed offspring to some degree.[23] And although Mrs. Roberts deeply resented the presence of Mahalia and her children, Mr. Roberts cared enough to keep the family intact, although some one hundred miles removed.

Notwithstanding the murky bi-racial relationships in the Old South, Quinton Roberts eventually returned to West Tennessee where he met and married Alice Walker, an "excellent seamstress" who "never worked on the plantation."[24] Because of her light skin, Alice enjoyed the "mulatto advantage"[25] and served primarily as a housekeeper. Her close proximity to and constant interaction with whites in the Walker household had furnished Alice the privileges of better food, better clothing, and literacy.

The union of Quinton and Alice produced ten children, one of whom was Mollie. Unlike Annie C. Tuggle's devout Methodist paternal grandfather, her maternal grandfather aligned himself with the Seventh Day Adventist Church. Like Charles Tuggle, Quinton Roberts, after purchasing eighty acres of land from his father, amassed enough resources to support his large family.[26]

The blood of the Tuggle and Roberts families converged in the veins of Annie C. Tuggle through her parents, Haywood Tuggle and Mollie Roberts. Determined to educate his children for a better future, Charles Tuggle sent Haywood to study at Rust College, a historically black college established by the Freedman's Aid Society of the Methodist Episcopal Church in Holly Springs, Mississippi, in 1866.[27] The father defrayed all his son's expenses, but for Haywood, romance superseded education. He took his father's hard-earned money, splurged it on a new wardrobe, and returned home to marry his childhood sweetheart, Mollie Roberts, on January 4, 1883.[28] Haywood's defiant spirit evidently rubbed off on young Annie, for as a teenager she ran away to Memphis, Tennessee, against her mother's stern warning, and her stubbornness and feisty temper often led her to defy authority throughout her life. Despite Haywood's deviation from his father's designs, he obviously made a happy decision. His delightful marriage to Mollie produced nine children and lasted fifty-seven years. This stable family life provided Annie and her siblings with a secure foundation in a rapidly changing and viciously racist world.

The Tuggle household, however, did know both turmoil and hardship. One spring morning in 1894, Annie's mother, while attending to her infant child, discovered that her father-in-law's house was engulfed with flames. She screamed, "Haywood, your daddy's house is on fire! Get up and run, run, run." Dashing over to his father's house, Haywood safely led his parents and sister, Sophia, out of the burning dwelling. This experience left an indelible mark on four-year-old Annie, who witnessed her grandparents' unspeakable grief. "Grandma cried and cried and how it did hurt me to see her cry. So I cried too, but not about the burning of the house. It hurt my feelings to see grandma cry as she did."[29]

Haywood's subsequent investigation into the fire suggested arson and pointed to Aunt Sophia's estranged husband as the culprit. Over the next several days, an observant and precocious Annie noticed that her parents had "close conversations" and the children "were not allowed to hear what was said." After many years, Annie's mother confessed that she had to "talk to your daddy day and night to keep him from hurting someone." Annie was relieved and proud that her mother "succeeded" in calming her enraged father and that "she was such a help to my father when he needed her most." While Mollie's words to her husband remain shrouded, one can safely conjecture that she sternly counseled him not to seek revenge because "God don't like ugly."[30] Mollie, together with countless other black women of faith, believed firmly that God would eventually repay all evildoers. Annie locked away this horrific event "in my heart, never to be forgotten."[31]

Even though Annie considered her father "brave," "daring," and "the greatest person in the world," her mother clearly left the most lasting impression on her young life. Mollie molded Annie and her siblings through prayer, wisdom, and encouragement. Because of two previous difficult childbirths, Mollie prayed to God daily to "enable her to pull through at the birth of her unborn child," Annie. In later life Annie connected her mother's experience with the biblical matriarch, Hannah, who prayed to God for deliverance from barrenness. "From this very act of my mother praying to God while I was yet in the making, I can never forget she gave me something that time nor eternity can erase."[32]

Annie's relationship with her mother bore a strong vein of friendship. Annie often wrote that she and her mother "talked together as friends and not as mother and daughter." This relationship served well when Earnest Carter, a tall, handsome, brown-skinned young man, expressed interest in fourteen-year-old Annie; her mother was unimpressed because he was "born out of wedlock." Mollie advised her daughter to rethink a future with Earnest, since her "children would not know who their grandfather was." Annie, who looked to her own paternal grandfather for emotional, material, and spiritual security, heeded her mother's advice and called off the courtship. Since mystery and miscegenation muddled Mollie's own family history, she well understood that cognizance of one's family background imparted a sense of security and self-assurance in an insecure milieu.

In addition to dispensing wisdom to Annie and her siblings, Mollie also lavished praise on them. In 1918, when leaders of a Church of Christ in Germantown asked Annie to say a few words to the congregation after the service, her mother came to her, shook her hand, and said: "Ann, I am thankful to have a daughter like you. I enjoyed what you had to say." Her mother's encouragement and approbation inspired Annie to "try harder each day of my life to be pleasing in the sight of God."[33] While Annie appreciated Mollie's wisdom and commendation, it was her discovery that her mother prayed for her before birth that compelled Annie to exclaim: "I owe her a debt of gratitude that can never be paid."[34] When reflecting on her life at age eighty-three, Annie acknowledged: "When I look back over my childhood training and realize what my mother did for me, I can never thank her enough for her love and obedience to God for doing the best she knew to bring up her children in the fear and admonition of the Lord."[35]

In essence, Annie Tuggle's family life proved a source of enduring strength and stability in her viscerally anti-black and widely misogynic society. From her paternal grandfather, Charles Tuggle, she inherited a rich spiritual foundation, a middle-class economic status, and a defiant spirit. From her maternal grandfather, Quinton Roberts, she acquired a legacy of determination and literacy buttressed by a thirst for knowledge. These priceless qualities catapulted young Annie into a white-dominated society and a male-controlled religious establishment with a sense of hope, determination, and gratitude. Most importantly, Mollie Tuggle's fervent prayers, wise counsel, and religious devotion had the most profound impact on Annie's life. And what her mother had been for her, Annie in turn became that and more for others—a prayerful advocate, a church leader, a Christian educator and historian, and a trustworthy advisor to both white and black leaders in Churches of Christ.

CHAPTER 2

"IF I HAD TEN THOUSAND VOICES"

The Burden of Education

"If the educated colored woman has a burden, and we believe she has— what is that burden?...What it is can be readily seen perhaps better than told, for it constantly annoys to irritation; it bulges out as did the load of Bunyan's Christian ignorance with its inseparable companions, shame and crime and prejudice."[1]

–Lucy Craft Laney
(1899)

African American women in the late nineteenth and early twentieth centuries collectively bore multiple burdens. In 1899 Lucy Craft Laney, a black educator from Georgia, stood before black teachers at the Hampton Negro Conference in Hampton, Virginia, and discussed the varied burdens black female instructors shouldered after emancipation. The enslavement of black people demoralized their families; thus, by instructing black youth to become efficient homemakers and hygienic caretakers, Laney believed that the "crushing burden of immorality which has its root in the disregard of the marriage vow, can be lightened. It must be, and the educated colored woman can and will do her part in lifting this burden." Laney saw untidy and unclean homes as "incubators of sin," leading to both "intellectual and moral death." In addition to the burden of eradicating immorality, black educators carried the burden of disseminating knowledge among a "people ignorant of the laws of nature and common decency." The heaviest burdens, however, were racism and misogyny since the strong imposed them on the weak and rendered them ubiquitous. "No one suffers under the weight of this burden," explained Laney, "as the educated Negro woman does; and she must help to lift it."[2] For Laney, then, black women teachers across the Deep South bore the dual responsibilities of stamping out immorality and ignorance among African Americans, while grappling with the ever-present problem of pervasive racism.

Annie C. Tuggle devised her plan to educate black children two years before Laney's rousing speech. At age seven, Annie attended the Featherton School in Shelby County, Tennessee, where instructor R. H. Neville, upon learning she was already literate, asked her to take her classmates outside and teach them their letters and numbers. Thrilled about the opportunity to interact with fellow students, Annie felt certain that they all knew the English alphabet and Arabic numerals. She was deeply disappointed to discover that the "little things could not count even to twenty." "I was one hurt soul," she admitted dejectedly. After asking the students why they could not read or write, they explained that their parents were illiterate. "Right then and there,"

Annie determined "to be a teacher the rest of my life and help little children to learn something for themselves."[3]

Tuggle kept her promise to become an educator, but a decade later her life radically changed when she converted from Methodism to Churches of Christ. In 1908, when spending her summer vacation with her sister Gertrude and her husband, Joe Holmes, both members of Churches of Christ, Annie embraced the tenets of this religious fellowship. Holmes's emphasis on personal Bible study and baptism for the remission of sins—based on his understanding of Acts 2:38—swayed young Annie. Her sister further explained that "there was no such thing as getting religion. 'Religion is a duty to perform'"—based on James 1:27. Their practice of substantiating assertions with biblical references deeply impressed Annie. "Now these simple facts read from the Bible were so striking and reasonable that I could not help believing them."[4] During the summer of 1908, seventeen-year-old Annie heard Henry Garrett enunciate the "plan of salvation,"[5] submitted to baptism, and "rose from the watery grave of baptism with a clear understanding that in order to please God I would have to study to show myself approved to Him, a workman that needeth not to be ashamed," a reference to 2 Timothy 2:15.[6] Tuggle's commitment to God and Churches of Christ, however, did not derail her educational pursuits. Her religious convictions only intensified her thirst for knowledge as well as her desire to illuminate the hearts and minds of black children.

A few months after her religious transition, Annie, with Gertrude's support and generosity, enrolled at Lane College in Jackson, Tennessee. Founded by Bishop Isaac Lane, a former slave of bi-racial ancestry, Lane College began offering classes from first grade through high school with college preparation courses and a teacher's degree program in 1882.[7] When Annie matriculated from the Colored Methodist Episcopal–controlled school, she was a seventeen-year-old eighth grader. Upon arriving on the college campus, Annie, having been reared on a spacious five hundred acre farm, expected to see several large and lavish buildings with "green grass, lovely flowers and evergreen shade trees." She was disappointed, however, to see "only two brick buildings standing on a small lot!"[8]

The friendliness of the almost 450 students,[9] most of whom boarded from Mississippi, Arkansas, and Tennessee, compensated for the shortcomings of the physical environment. School officials initially assigned Annie to the eighth grade, but she was demoted because of her inability to do the work, acknowledging that rural school districts in West Tennessee sometimes employed ill-prepared teachers. Annie's demotion to the seventh grade was a blessing in disguise, however, for the class proved to be a better fit for her, and she met a "wonderful" teacher, L. M. Burns.[10]

Supervisors of the girls' dormitory soon made Annie monitor of her dining hall table. One morning after all the students had eaten breakfast, an upper-class student asked Annie what happened to the plate of biscuits on the table. Annie replied frankly and plainly: "Miss Osborne *taken* one, Miss Griffith *taken* one or two and I *taken* some." Upon hearing Annie's improper grammar, the student's facial expression fell and she exclaimed: "Miss Tuggle, please don't ever murder English like that any more while you live. You should have said, 'Miss Osborne *took* one, Miss Griffith *took* one or two and I *took* some.'"[11] With a blend of humor and humility, Annie accepted the upper-classman's correction and spent most of her time at Lane College mastering English grammar and literature.

All upper-classmen at Lane College were not as cordial, however. Some high school and college students displayed a "superior attitude" toward the elementary students; the former even mocking those who associated with lower grade students. But the tension between students at the Methodist school may well have stemmed from the "color complex," many light-skinned and dark-skinned African Americans acutely and mutually discriminated against each other. Indeed, the Colored Methodist Episcopal Church was often criticized for not appointing bishops of darker hue. Young Annie became ensnared in this color and class conflict at Lane College.[12] Annie further felt out of place as a seventeen-year-old student in the seventh grade, resenting the sting of rejection. But she overcame this awkwardness by making friends with Allie Osborne and Matilda Griffith. Jeroy Meacham, a tall and handsome high school student, expressed interest in Annie and asked to escort her to a church social in Jackson, Tennessee. Meacham, "as polite as a basket of chips," was a splendid entertainer, an aspiring doctor, and, most importantly, he made Annie feel like a "college girl already."[13]

Annie's courtship with Jeroy Meacham and her stay at Lane College proved temporary. She badly missed her family in West Tennessee and the class tension she experienced on campus deeply disturbed her. "The superior attitude of the students at

Lane," Annie explained to her mother, was "very serious . . . the upper-class students thought that they better than the grade students, and there was very little fellowship between them."[14] While there might have been tension between light-skinned and dark-skinned, urban and rural, students at Lane College, Annie's own evolving theological convictions that the Methodist Church was the "devil's work" probably influenced her to withdraw from Lane College and return home.[15]

Despite leaving Lane College, Annie insisted to her mother that she would finish her education and become a "first-rate teacher." But Annie wanted to transfer to the nearby LeMoyne Normal Institute in Memphis. Her mother sternly objected: "No, I don't want you to go to Memphis to live. At 19, you are just the right age to be led astray."[16] Mollie Tuggle believed her daughter had good intentions, but she was deeply concerned about the "white slave trade," the sexual exploitation of girls believed to be prevalent in Memphis.

Mollie Tuggle's apprehension for her daughter's safety stemmed from flaws inherent in the nation's burgeoning urbanization. In 1907 Congress, responding to the increasing and alarming reports from muckraking journalists about "white slavery," appointed a commission to investigate the charges of the "importation of women for immoral purposes." The commission found that the entrapment of young women into prostitution was indeed a major problem in cities across America.[17] Both journalists and playwrights helped promote concern for the "sisters in sin"; in the first two decades of the twentieth century, New York City alone produced fifty plays featuring prostitutes.[18] The most effective means of spreading anxiety over white trafficking, however, were white-slave tracts, such as "The Great War on White Slavery," "The Cruel and Inhuman Treatment of White Slaves," and a number of others, which portrayed innocent country girls as victims to insidious white slavers of the city.[19] Reformers, however, worked diligently to shield white "delinquent daughters" from sexual predators; but, young black women such as Annie C. Tuggle had only their loving mothers as aides in resisting the lure of sexual perversion.[20]

Sexual promiscuity apparently ran rampant in Memphis in the early twentieth century. Seven thousand professional sinners, most of whom were prostitutes, resided in Shelby County.[21] The two main prostitution streets, Hadden Avenue and Gayoso Street, cut through the heart of black Memphis where W. C. Handy's blues and "red light districts" flourished. One Memphis minister testified, "It seems that the devil left hell on a vacation, stopped over at Memphis, sat down on Beale Street and rewrote the Ten Commandments leaving the NOT out of each Commandment."[22] Mollie Tuggle obviously imbibed such reports and vigorously opposed her daughter's plan to transfer to LeMoyne Normal Institute in Memphis, convinced that it was the "wrong place to send a girl to college."[23]

However, Annie Tuggle's independent "make up" prevailed, and she went to Memphis against her mother's wishes and found lodging with her Aunt Sophia. When her father came to retrieve her, Sophia said: "Haywood, that gal is just like Paw . . . she has a head of her own and we can't do anything with her. She is likely to leave us and we may never see her again. So if you let her stay here with me, I will bear all the expenses and let her go to LeMoyne, since she is so determined to go to school."[24] Haywood consented, and a joyful Annie entered a new school even as Aunt Sophia laid down rigid guidelines for her niece, demanding that she "come straight home from school every day."[25]

Annie found the LeMoyne Normal Institute vastly different from Lane College. At the former, boys and girls sat together, hit each other over the head playfully, and were "very noisy but quite sociable." The Memphis school encouraged a greater sense of equality—"no big 'I's' and little 'U's.'" Smaller than that of Lane College, the LeMoyne student body was "very friendly." When the two schools competed against each other in a baseball game, Annie delighted that her new school prevailed. Despite the many friendships she nurtured in Memphis, she judged the school inferior with not "enough to offer to encourage me to set a higher aim in life."[26]

In the spring of 1910, Annie took and passed the Shelby County teachers' examination and then became an assistant teacher at the Prospect School in Germantown, Tennessee, working with first through third graders. Annie taught under the supervision of her cousin Eunice Roberts, to whom she confessed daily her desire to earn a college degree and become a "number one good teacher."[27] Eunice, touched by her cousin's hunger for learning, vowed to send her to college and pay her "expenses out of my own money because you are so anxious to go."[28]

When the Prospect School closed for the cotton-picking season, ending Annie's brief tenure there, she learned of another opening in west Tennessee. Upon receiving a recommendation letter from a prominent white friend of the family, Squire Kimbrough, Annie became principal of the Promised Land School at Millington, Tennessee. Dr. Chambus, the school's director, gave Annie the position of principal because he did not want "any Memphis 'trash' to ruin the community and teach children nothing."[29] Presiding over a school with 115 students in first through six grades, Annie felt the heavy weight of daily instruction as well as the challenge of living a morally upright life. When Enoch Weakly, an eighteen-year-old student, offered to escort her to her boarding room, Annie politely yet firmly declined. Taking her inspiration from the biblical characters Joseph and Daniel, she scrupulously monitored her every step to "give no occasion to the devil," a reference to 1 Timothy 5:14.[30] Young Annie understood that her individual and private actions affected her reputation at school and in the broader black community.

In 1911, Annie replaced her cousin Eunice as principal at the Prospect School in Germantown. A former classmate from LeMoyne, Susie Trueheart, assisted her there. Susie herself bore the burden of grief because of the recent death of her mother and assumed the added responsibility of caring for her four-year-old sister, Wendell. Annie candidly admitted that even though Susie, who held a high school diploma and a teaching certificate, was "better qualified than I," she "respected my position as principal." Humbled by the more than one hundred students under her care and an assistant teacher with higher qualifications, Annie spent many sleepless nights reflecting on how to "better my condition."[31]

During this period of uncertainty for Annie, G. P. Bowser, a preacher and principal of the Silver Point Christian Institute in Silver Point, Tennessee, seventy-five miles east of Nashville, came to Capleville, near Germantown, and conducted a gospel meeting. He met Annie and urged her to enroll at his school and complete her high school education. Like Annie, Bowser had been a devout Methodist before converting to the Stone-Campbell Movement under the guidance of Sam Davis. Well trained and well versed in several languages, Bowser established the Silver Point Christian Institute in 1907 and housed it at the Jackson Street Church of Christ facility in Nashville. Two years later Bowser relocated his school to Silver Point, and in 1913 Annie enrolled in the ninth grade, studying Bible, Algebra, English, History, and Latin. Like other Silver Point students who worked to defray their expenses, Annie served as a cook to pay her tuition. She delighted in her daily chores, believing that "God was pleased with me for helping a person like Bro. Bowser."[32]

Annie deeply admired both G. P. Bowser and his wife, Fannie, calling her a "jewel," a splendid housekeeper, and one who could "make something out of nothing." In Annie's opinion, Fannie was indispensable to her husband's work as an educator. According to G. P. Bowser's biographer, however, Mrs. Bowser troubled the marriage with her "very hot temper" which often erupted in her husband's presence. When frustrated, Fannie fumed and fussed so loudly that her anger was felt and heard throughout the two-story building that housed the Silver Point Christian Institute.[33]

Annie knew firsthand the difficulty of mastering a boiling temper since she struggled with this herself. When a dispute occurred between students at the Silver Point Christian Institute, the principal intervened and squashed the argument. He then warned: "Sister Annie, I can see from your make up that you are destined to become one of the greatest women in our brotherhood, but you will have to curb your temper. I don't condemn for having a temper—I am glad you have it; but you should control it, and not let it control you." Annie called the rebuke one of the "worst whippings that I have ever had, but I took it in the same spirit in which it was given—the Spirit of Christ."[34]

Like many black women of her era, Tuggle's rage proved both a blessing and a curse. Ida B. Wells's "besetting sin" was her feisty temper, yet it fired her passion to stamp out lynching in North America.[35] Fannie Lou Hamer struggled to subdue her anger, but it inspired her crusade against racial discrimination and political disfranchisement in Mississippi and beyond.[36] On a more personal level, Annie Tuggle's temper churned within her, fostering a spirit of impatience and perhaps leading to her failed marriage; yet her ire also repelled unscrupulous black suitors and white sexual predators.

More significantly, Annie Tuggle's fiery disposition fueled her drive to canvass for the Silver Point Christian Institute and to champion the cause of Christian education for black youth. In 1914 Annie assumed the task of fundraising for Bowser's school, traversing the southern states with hopes of transforming the fledgling school into a strong and stable institution like Fisk University in Nashville. The following year when Booker T. Washington died, many black leaders in the Churches of Christ, such as Samuel Robert Cassius, lamented their hero's demise. Cassius, an African American preacher and "race man" from Oklahoma, lauded Washington as a "natural orator," "a deep thinker," and "a convincing speaker" who both inspired people and was himself stimulated to "higher and greater" feats by white philanthropists. Tuggle also applauded the Tuskegee Wizard for his tenacity and determination, "convinced that it was his will power that enabled Mr. Washington to accomplish such a great work."[37]

Tuggle imbibed the educational philosophies of both Booker T. Washington and G. P. Bowser. For Tuggle, however, the most significant difference between Washington's Tuskegee Institute and Bowser's Silver Point Christian Institute was that the latter sought "to educate the head and hands of the negro, *plus* his heart, and prepare him for this world and the world to come." She further argued that industrial education was insufficient stating, "The negro still stands outside the ark of safety, unprepared to meet his God, without even a knowledge of the teaching of Christ or what the Lord requires of him to inherit eternal life." Biblical instruction and spiritual training must accompany industrial knowledge to curb immorality and racial violence. Tuggle called on whites in Churches of Christ to aid the black American "by having God's word sounded out to him in its purity, which teaches him that, denying ungodliness and worldly lust, he should live soberly, righteously, and godly in this present world. When this is done, the prison bars will be less needed and the visitations of the mob will not be so frequent." She also mildly rebuked Cassius and others in Churches of Christ for their failure to support Bowser's educational efforts and challenged them to "fall in line" with the

Silver Point Christian Institute and "stick to it" as Washington "stuck to" his Alabama enterprise.[38]

Her fundraising tours revealed to Tuggle a disheartening truth about those she visited. In the spring of 1916, Tuggle voiced her increasing frustration with the spiritual plight of African Americans. "When I go into the various homes and the different localities of my people and see how ignorant they are of the holy Scriptures which are able to make them wise unto salvation," she lamented, "my heart almost melts within me." Many black people who had acquired a liberal arts education, Tuggle believed, were as "ignorant of the Bible as an infant." The remedy for biblical illiteracy, in her estimation, lay in "Bible schools" such as the Silver Point Christian Institute. "I believe if we had a real Bible school where our people could be given a Bible training together with their literacy and industrial training, ignorance would be pressed to the wall and the blessed spirit of the Savior would have a home in our hearts." She vowed to remain agitated and restless until she saw a "real Bible school among my people and the students going forth as burning lamps."[39] Despite her best efforts, however, the Silver Point Christian Institute collapsed in 1918 because of insufficient monetary support and a dwindling student population whose parents joined the widening stream of southern blacks flowing northward in the first Great Migration during World War I.[40]

After the failure of the Silver Point Christian Institute, G. P. Bowser and Annie Tuggle moved in separate directions. Bowser relocated to Louisville, Kentucky, to plant a church there while Tuggle returned to her home in West Tennessee. When talking things over with her friend and mother, Annie deplored the closing of Bowser's school, yet joked that the town of Silver Point had many "points" where the school was located, but not much "silver." "We both laughed," she continued, "and I kept on with my story by saying that Brother and Sister Bowser had done a marvelous work at Silver Point for the chance they had." Tuggle's ability to find humor amid discouraging circumstances not only attested unflagging resolve, but it also demonstrated how African Americans survived life in the segregated South. James Weldon Johnson captured the therapeutic effect humor had on African Americans, noting that "I have since learned that this ability to laugh heartily is, in part, the salvation of the American Negro; it does much to keep him from going the way of the Indian."[41] This insightful observation certainly applies to Tuggle and many other contemporary African Americans across the Jim Crow South.

More seriously, her mother contemplated donating "twenty or twenty-five acres of land," if it relocated to Germantown, Tennessee. While Annie engaged in "deep conversations" with her mother, the philanthropist A. M. Burton sent a letter inviting her to serve as a field agent and teacher for the newly established Southern Practical Institute in Nashville. The school, scheduled to open on January 5, 1920, would train students in liberal arts as well as in domestic and industrial trades. Burton's enclosed generous check left Tuggle and her mother "speechless." Annie accepted, eagerly interpreting the gift as a "great blessing that came to refresh, encourage and inspire the people of God through Bro. Burton."[42]

On opening day, excitement filled the air on the campus of the Southern Practical Institute with its three-story building of forty rooms accommodating forty black students. A. M. Burton appointed C. E. W. Dorris, a white educator, as superintendent and G. P. Bowser as principal, and assigned Annie Tuggle to teach the sixth grade. Three of Annie's students, R. N. Hogan, Sutton Johnson, and T. W. Rucks, would mature to become influential and renowned preachers in Churches of Christ. Annie had a "heart-to-heart talk" with her class, challenging them to be a "blessing" to themselves, to their communities, and to God. Her students "seemed encouraged and gave me a big, lovely smile."[43]

Annie planned to make the Southern Practical Institute her "permanent home and get a Christian education in this same school by attending night classes." The opportunity seemed a dream come true, but the school suddenly closed six weeks later because of a "gross misunderstanding, never to open again!" Racial tension destroyed the new school. C. E. W. Dorris, the white superintendent, demanded that black students enter the schoolhouse through the back door, a custom prevalent across the New South,[44] but G. P. Bowser vehemently opposed the practice in this school for blacks, viewing it as a gesture of humiliation to the students.[45] The Dorris–Bowser conflict demonstrates how deeply the undercurrents of racism ran even among white Christians who worked to benefit their black fellows.[46]

The Southern Practical Institute's collapse devastated Tuggle. "If this had been a material crash one could have heard it for miles and miles away, but it was deep and dreadful and crushed the souls and hearts of the ones who were concerned."[47] Yet in spite of the school's closure, she clung passionately to her desire to educate African Americans. "It pains my heart from day to day as I think of the present condition that is existing throughout the brotherhood on account of untrained leadership; and if I had ten thousand voices, I would lift up every one in behalf of a Christian institution; if I had ten thousand times ten thousand lives to live, I would spend each one for the salvation and education of my people."[48] Tuggle bore the self-assumed burden of training young people for leadership roles in Churches of Christ.

Despite the failure of both the Silver Point Christian Institute and the Southern Practical Institute, Tuggle decided to remain in Nashville, "the Athens of the South, and get a college education if it cost my life."[49] She enrolled at Walden University, established as Central Tennessee College by the Freedman's Aid Society of the Methodist Episcopal Church in 1866, and completed her high school diploma there. White and black Christians in Nashville helped sustain Tuggle when she later entered Walden's college program. S. P. Pittman, a white instructor at the Nashville Bible School (later Lipscomb University), defrayed her tuition and arranged her daily bus fare. An affable and affluent black couple, P. H. and Millie Black, housed Annie and two other Walden University students, Freddie M. Brandon and Mary Allen. Black was a skilled brick layer and his wife a "professional seamstress" and an excellent housekeeper. Because of the generosity of these believers in Nashville as well as her own diligence and determination, Annie graduated in 1923 from Walden University with her college degree as valedictorian of her class at the mature age of thirty-three.[50]

Annie Tuggle, a perennial non-traditional student, excelled in a traditional academic environment. Although she felt out of place as an older student learning and interacting with younger and less mature classmates, her drive and hunger for knowledge stretched her vision beyond any discomfort and helped her focus on the prize of a college education. As an aspiring educator, Tuggle bore the multiple burdens of educating herself, subduing her anger, equipping black youth, leading better qualified teachers, and grappling with the failure of two black Church of Christ schools. Yet Tuggle mastered these difficulties in gaining a Christian education, acquiring her first grade teaching certificate, and earning her high school diploma and college degree. Such impressive accomplishments proved a double-edged sword, however. Her academic training cast her into leadership roles among women older than she as well as men who were the presumed leaders in society and in her church. Better trained than most men society designated as her superiors, Tuggle, although now academically established, remained restless and continued to seek a fulfilling place of Christian service.

PART II

THE BURDEN OF GENDER

1924–1968

The staff of Hamner Taylor Elementary School, 1925.
Annie C. Tuggle is seated in the middle.

CHAPTER 3

"AND YOU WILL BE THE ONE LYNCHED"

The Burdens of Sex, Marriage, and Divorce

"The color of her face alone is sufficient invitation to the Southern white man. . . . Few colored girls reach the age of sixteen without receiving advances from them—maybe from a young 'upstart,' and often from a man old enough to their father, a white haired veteran of sin."[1]

—A Southern Colored Woman (1904)

Black enslaved mothers remained ever vigilant of their adolescent daughters in the horrific environment of white sexual predators on southern plantations and beyond. "The mother of slaves is very watchful," testified Harriet Jacobs, an enslaved African from Edenton, North Carolina. "She knows there is no security for her children. After they have entered their teens she lives in daily expectation of trouble."[2] Jacobs constantly resisted the sexual advances of her owner, Dr. James Norcom, and as a teenager, she was seduced into carnal relations with Samuel

Tredwell Sawyer, a North Carolina Congressman, who sired her two children. Hence, Jacobs knew from personal experience the double burdens of racism and sexism that enslaved women shouldered. "Slavery is terrible for men; but it is far more terrible for women," she explained. "Superadded to the burden common to all, *they* have wrongs, and sufferings, and mortifications peculiarly their own."[3]

A brutal Civil War and the passage of the Thirteenth Amendment abolished black chattel enslavement but did not eradicate the tenacious effects of racism and sexism. Long after slavery's demise, unscrupulous white men in the South continued with impunity to violate black women sexually. In 1904 a southern black woman reported that a white gentleman offered her a school directorship "if I did his bidding." She further lamented watching her own daughters grow up, realizing, "Where the white girl has one temptation, mine will have many."[4] Eight years later, another black woman from the South revealed that she was fired from her housekeeping job after she "shoved" away her white employer who impudently hugged and kissed her. Infuriated, the black woman told her husband about the unsolicited advance, but when the black man confronted his wife's former employer, the white man cursed him, slapped him, and had him jailed. The judge then fined the black plaintiff twenty-five dollars. The harassed woman lamented that black females in the South "are but little more than pack horses, beasts of burden, slaves!"[5]

The plethora of testimonies from such black southern women underscores the tragic reality that "slavery by another name" flourished long after the Civil War. "White men openly forced black slaves into their beds for two centuries before the Civil War, and sexual access to local black women remained a running point of confrontation between white landowners and their black laborers deep into the twentieth century—a phenomenon that continued to demonstrate itself a century later with the public revelation that South Carolina senator Strom Thurmond" raped a black servant girl in 1925, fathering a child with her.[6] Three decades later, an eleven-year-old Endesha Ida Mae Holland worked for the white Lawrence family in Greenwood, Mississippi, where Mrs. Lawrence callously arranged for her husband to rape her. Reflecting on the incident several years later, Holland, who emerged as a civil rights activist and went on to earn a PhD scathingly marveled that "the white man's great dream, his burning desire" was to "have sex with a colored woman."[7] Many black children shared Holland's plight in the 1950s South as such leading white families maintained a level of morality dealing with blacks which would have earned lengthy jail sentences had white children been involved.

Mollie Tuggle, a product of an illicit bi-racial union in the Old South, knew fully what black girls were up against in the New South, so she constantly counseled her five daughters about the prospect of sexual violence. When daughter Annie organized a small congregation of women in Germantown, Tennessee, she named it the Smyrna Church of Christ, after one of the seven churches in Asia mentioned in the Book of Revelation with whom the "Lord found no fault." As the congregation increased, black and white Christians in nearby Memphis collaborated and invited a white preacher to conduct a gospel meeting. After one of the night services, the preacher "touched a string of beads that I was wearing without even thinking of anything but the good work that was in progress." When Annie got home, her mother fumed that "something went on under the tent tonight that I certainly did not like." What young Annie viewed as an innocent act of a white Christian man admiring her bit of jewelry, her mother understood as an inappropriate gesture that could result in a lynching. "I saw that white preacher with his hands on the beads you were wearing around your neck," thundered Mollie, "and before you know anything, there will be a lynching scrape right here in Germantown and you will be the one lynched."[8]

Mollie understood the complex "culture of segregation in the South,"[9] perceiving that many southern whites branded black men as rapists and black women as promiscuous, fired by the "embodiment of passion," even as they held up white women as pure, innocent, and virtuous. "By creating a mythological black Venus and a white Virgin Mary," historians Mary Frances Berry and John W. Blassingame have insisted, "the white man dehumanized both."[10] Cole Blease, governor of South Carolina from 1910 to 1915, spoke for many white southerners and sent a clear message to lecherous young whites such as the aforementioned Strom Thurmond when he asserted: "I have . . . very serious doubt as to whether the crime of rape can be committed upon a negro."[11] Even had the white preacher's gesture been innocent, Mollie understood that her black daughter would be deemed the culprit.

Mollie Tuggle also recognized that most whites in southern Churches of Christ imbibed much of the racism ingrained in American culture. After emancipation, whites in the Stone-Campbell Movement openly expressed a belief in African Americans' so-called inferiority and often characterized them as generally lazy. In the summer of 1868, C. Kendrick, a resident of Bastrop, Texas, wrote of former enslaved Africans as an "indolent, thoughtless people . . . with very small aspirations to anything beyond the poorest food and raiment." A dozen years later, J. W. Crenshaw, a native of Cadiz, Kentucky, labeled southern blacks as "ignorant and superstitious."[12]

Whites in Churches of Christ during the Progressive era displayed a degree of ambivalence toward African Americans. On the one hand, John M. McCaleb, a white preacher from Tennessee and missionary to Japan, insisted in 1907 that southern blacks required proper education since their language was "awful, and his thought crude and disconnected." He then chided white Christians who warmly welcomed Europeans and Asians into their schools and churches, but rudely spurned the "American African." McCaleb proposed that white administrators of Church of Christ schools partner with such black colleges as Fisk University and Tuskegee Institute to teach African Americans "'professionally,' but not socially." He further called on his white fellows to recognize the humanity of black people, arguing that the "black man, though black, is a man, a member of the great human family, and that he has rights which should be duly respected. He should be dealt with and in every way treated as a man."[13]

On the other hand, McCaleb cautioned black southerners to stay in their "place" and realize the "vast difference between them and us." African Americans, according to McCaleb, hated their own physical appearance, their "black skin," "flattened nose," and "kinky hair." "I do not blame them for this," he explained, "but let us remember that this difference in race is the work of God and not of man." A true paternalist, McCaleb advised blacks to "cease their silly and seemly efforts" to try to be like white people and to "avoid intruding on the feelings of others." Like many southern whites, McCaleb feared that if given an opportunity to interact freely with whites, black men would enjoy "making love to our daughters and will seek a place in the social circle."[14] Just as McCaleb and many southerners detested and prevented on pain of death black men from freely mixing with their white women, black mothers such as Mollie Tuggle distrusted white men who interacted with their black daughters.

Mollie Tuggle knew as well that lynchings were common across the New South, for between 1889 and 1918, white mobs barbarously murdered at least 2,522 African Americans. Fifty women were numbered among the slain.[15] In the 1890s a white mob in San Antonio, Texas, sealed a black woman in a barrel, drove long sharpened nails through the sides, and rolled it up and down a hill until she was a bloody corpse. In 1918 a savage rabble in Valdosta, Georgia, burned alive Mary Turner, together with her unborn child.[16] Mollie Tuggle, with all black mothers, understood all too well that she could not look to the legal system or white believers, even those in her own religious brotherhood,[17] to protect her daughter from lynch mobs across the South. Black daughters would have to rely on their own vigilance and common sense for survival.

The white preacher's motive notwithstanding, Annie took her mother's warning to heart, attributing lynchings in the New South to demonic activity. "If people keep their minds on evil things all the time and never accept the good, the devil will finally get the upper hand and there will be lynching and every other kind of evil work. So the meeting soon closed and everything worked out smoothly and I did not wear the beads again."[18]

As early as her ninth year, Annie Tuggle had envisioned being a wife and mother of six children, five boys and one girl. Her dream of becoming a wife came true on July 27, 1927, when she married Dr. John Waller, a native of Brownsville, Tennessee, and a graduate of Meharry Medical College. Waller, too, grew up in Churches of Christ and was Annie's high school classmate at Walden University. Because they shared the same religious heritage as well as a similar educational background, the newlyweds confidently believed they would have no "trouble in the home, religiously."[19]

Shortly after their marriage, the Wallers relocated to Cincinnati, Ohio, where John opened a pharmacy. They had joined a stream of black southerners flowing to northern cities in search of better economic, social, and educational opportunities.[20] In 1928 alone, the black population in Ohio soared from 186,187 to 309,304.[21] That same year the African American population in Cincinnati reached approximately 35,000.[22] Black Americans who fled the South soon discovered, however, that the Queen City was no "Promised Land." White racism in Cincinnati barred blacks from local theaters, confined black women to the domestic sphere, and restricted entire black families to ghettoes and slums with poor plumbing and insanitary conditions. Careful research has revealed, "Racism and discrimination were present in almost every facet of black life in Cincinnati."[23] Catherine Brooks, a black migrant from Georgia, testified more poignantly: "Cincinnati wasn't all it was supposed to be. When I went home, and people said, what about Cincinnati? I said 'honey if you doing all right [in Georgia], then stay.'"[24]

Entangled in a true lover's knot with her groom, Annie Tuggle Waller viewed the Queen City more positively. The transition from Tennessee to Ohio was, for Annie, "like the discovery of a New World" with beautiful mountains, valleys, city parks, and well-learned people "from an educational point of view."[25] The most delightful part about living in Cincinnati was being with John. Annie deemed her husband "great," and his financial support of Annie in their brief marriage proved generous enough to sustain her "until this good day." John knew that he had married a special woman, complimenting her "broadmindedness to help those in need." More specifically, John expressed, "You are my wife and I am thankful for the business qualities you have."[26]

But the Stock Market Crash in 1929 and the ensuing Great Depression wiped out the resources of most Americans, especially black northerners.[27] The widening depression touched the Wallers in Cincinnati, Ohio. Annie, ever the optimist, believed that God would provide for their needs, finding comfort in one of her "pet Scriptures," Psalm 37:4, "Delight thyself also in the Lord; and he shall give thee the desires of thine heart." John agreed, but insisted that "one cannot just sit with his hands folded and wait for the Lord to hunt him up and supply his needs."[28] He insisted that human initiative must accompany God's activity.

Feeling the economic squeeze, Annie offered to assist her pharmacist husband financially by signing up new subscribers to the *Cincinnati Bulletin*, a black newspaper circulating in the Queen City. She was thrilled about the opportunity to win cash prizes, but John felt somewhat embarrassed that his wife, who "just married a doctor," would have to canvass the city enrolling subscribers. The practical Annie, citing Proverbs 16:18, "Pride goeth before destruction, and a haughty spirit before a fall," suggested, "It would be better for me to try to help you than to set [*sic*] here and see you fail and lose everything you have." John reluctantly consented to her wishes.[29]

Full of zeal and determination, Annie traversed the city of Cincinnati, made many friends, and enlisted many new readers. John generously contributed fifty dollars and told her to subscribe her mother, his mother, and other relatives whom "I saw fit to pay for." At the end of the six-week campaign, Annie won the second largest prize, a Plymouth Coupe. She and her husband sold the car for $650, paid off Waller's pressing medical bill of $275, and used the balance "to fix up the back room in the store for living quarters."[30]

Despite this joyous moment, the young couple, like other Americans, still felt the sting of the Great Depression. While many businesses in Cincinnati failed, John's Model Drug Store survived, even though suffering a "terrible blow." The sluggish economy spilled over into, and soured, the Waller's marriage.

Annie adored her husband, considering John a "loveable person." Yet in her view, greed flawed his makeup. "He loved money so well that he worshipped it," Annie lamented. "This love of money led him to fire the pharmacist who worked the night shift." To save money John worked both the day and night shifts until he completely exhausted himself; Annie could not convince him to value life more than money.[31]

"But worst of all," Annie bemoaned, "he did not want any children in the family." Even though Annie had dreamed of having a half-dozen children, John, like many Americans financially strapped and emotionally drained by the Great Depression, deliberately chose to avoid having children, since he struggled to feed his wife and himself. He convinced Annie to take steps to keep her childless. During the Great Depression, many American women who wanted no children used Lysol, a household cleaning product, as a douche. Lysol weakened blood vessels, caused spontaneous abortions, and intensified vascular problems.[32] The remedy, whether Lysol or a pharmaceutical concoction, adversely affected Annie's health, blotting out her childhood dream of mothering six children and sinking her into "almost a living death."[33]

Even though Annie never disclosed the specific medication her husband gave her, the episode damaged their brief marriage irreparably. The couple agreed to separate and eventually divorced in 1932. Annie proudly reclaimed her maiden name and never married again. To John's greed and selfishness must be added Annie's explosive temper, stubbornness, and independent spirit as factors working to sour the marriage. Carrying the burden of a failed marriage, Tuggle compared herself to the biblical matriarch, Naomi, who after the untimely deaths of her husband and two sons, returned home "sad, poor in spirit and a lack of necessary things of life." While Annie's ex-husband lived until 1960, she retreated to her home in "dear old Tennessee" where friends and family "like Naomi helped me."[34]

After her devastating divorce, Annie Tuggle had further unpleasant and complicated encounters with men, white men. In the early 1940s, she worked as a cotton-picker in Arkansas to support herself. On the first day an exhausted Annie rested briefly on her knees. But her white partner, Will, was infuriated and yelled, "I'm not going to have any resting on your knee today while you are picking with me; you see this belt, I'll take it off right now and wear you out with it." Threatened with a whipping, Annie hastily got off her knees, yet she defiantly challenged Will to "take his belt off right away and wear me out because I was going to pick cotton the way I chose to pick it without any dictation." Annie's fiery response to her partner's threat caused him to smile and apologize. "I forgave him and we got along nicely the rest of the day."[35] It is unclear whether Will was older or younger than Annie; nevertheless, he without question felt that his whiteness and maleness made him superior. But Annie courageously challenged his authority, no small feat in 1940s Arkansas.

The next day, Annie partnered with another white man, Fred, a fast cotton-picker and a seemingly nice man, who helped her get caught up with her rows when she fell behind. Fred, however, astonished Annie when he asked her "to leave the cotton patch awhile and go over to the woods and rest so we can talk to each other in quietness." He then flashed a "roll of money at me and smiled." Stunned and frightened, Annie sternly refused Fred's sexual advances, declaring, "It was so nice of you to help me keep my row up with yours. God will bless you for kindness." Expressing her deep commitment to God, Annie commended Fred's "loving mother," who trained him to be a fast cotton-picker and to "help others to work fast." Annie was unwilling to commit sexual immorality because of her desire to "rest in the presence of God and never have to pick any more cotton throughout eternity." Annie's rebuff and testimony silenced Fred who "picked cotton until quitting" without saying another word.[36]

The next day Annie picked cotton alone until the white overseer joined her. Without forewarning, the supervisor told Annie about his "turnip patch just around the corner of that skirt of the woods" and offered her as much as she wanted to take home. He then "winked his eye" at Annie and invited her to the "woods around the corner," but she spurned his offer "because I knew what he wanted." Annie did not see the overseer any more until the end of the day, when he weighed her cotton sack but refused to give her all her due pay "because I did not meet him in the turnip patch." Reflecting later on her experiences in the Arkansas cotton fields, Annie concluded that there was nothing wrong with the cotton patches, but only with "what comes from the homes." She knew, "If cotton pickers are not taught the right things at home, they will leave the field and go into the woods and engage in immoral acts."[37]

Annie Tuggle, a beautiful and attractive woman, carried a sharp tongue, feisty temper, and unwavering loyalty to God which prevailed over disrespectful co-workers and warded off potential sexual predators. Her experiences in an Arkansas cotton field confirm the findings of such scholars as Paula Giddings: "Sexual exploitation was so rampant that it compelled thousands of women to leave the South, or to urge their daughters to do so."[38] For Annie, however, the burdens of racism and sexism proved both onerous and ubiquitous. Her marriage to a black man failed during the Great Depression while she lived in the North. White men in the South sexually harassed and unscrupulously cheated her out of her earnings. Although never lynched by a white mob as her mother feared, Annie fended off sexual advances on at least three occasions. Paradoxically, it was her black ex-husband who left her with lingering emotional and physical scars by giving her unsafe medication to prevent her from having children. Despite these trials and tribulations, Annie, armed with an indefatigable commitment to moral purity, moved forward, convinced that "the word of the Lord is right and will endure forever."[39]

CHAPTER 4

A CHILDLESS MOTHER

The Burden of Leadership in African American Churches of Christ

"The inhabitants of the villages ceased,
they ceased in Israel, until that I Deborah arose,
that I arose a mother in Israel."

–JUDGES 5:7

"What if I am a woman; is not the God of ancient times
the God of these modern days?
Did he not raise up Deborah,
to be a mother, and a judge in Israel?
Did not queen Esther save the
lives of the Jews?"

–MARIA W. STEWART
(1835)

Financially depleted, emotionally depressed, and mentally drained because of her failed marriage, Annie C. Tuggle returned to her home in Germantown, Tennessee. She compared her anguish to that of the Old Testament matriarch Naomi who retreated "to her native home, sad, poor in spirit and a lack of the necessary things of life."[1] Yet her family came to her rescue in her time of despair, marital failure, and barrenness. "In my case," explained Tuggle, "my husband was not dead but estranged, and my hope for children which I had in early childhood, could never be a reality." Crushed beneath the burdens of rejection and disappointment, Tuggle relied on her biological and spiritual family in West Tennessee for support and sustenance. "True enough my friends and kinspeople like Naomi helped me."[2]

Not only did Tuggle receive emotional encouragement from her immediate family members, but she also gained spiritual uplift by pouring her heart and soul into the lives of young people whom she taught and mentored. In essence, even though Tuggle had no biological children, she became a spiritual mother and mentor to many youths in the schools and churches she served, thereby emerging as a leader in a religious fellowship that strictly excluded women from such a role. While studying at Tennessee A&I State College (later Tennessee State University), Tuggle came under the influence of George W. Gore, an English professor, who impressed her as a true leader. One morning Gore walked into an extremely noisy classroom. He stood silently at his desk for a while before firmly stating: "Young friends, this is a college class and not a kindergarten. You are supposed to know you are here to further prepare yourselves for your life's work." After Gore's firm, yet mild, rebuke the classroom fell completely silent. In Tuggle's opinion, her English professor demonstrated through his own teaching and conduct that true leadership was the "art of influencing people to cooperate toward some goal which they come to find desireable [sic]."[3] Tuggle never forgot Gore's leadership style, and she worked constantly to imitate him.

After her painful divorce from John Waller, her parents and especially her youngest sister, Emma (Tuggle) Rushing, proved to be her most diligent and sympathetic supporters. After failing to land a job in the Shelby County System, Emma encouraged Annie not to give up, reminding her that the "jobs do not belong to the ones who are over them, they belong to God. In due time you will get one." Emma and her husband, General Rushing, gave Annie wise counsel and free use of their car. More importantly, General introduced his sister-in-law to Squire Holman, an influential white businessman in Memphis. During their interview, Holman confessed that he had given his "uttermost" to get a teaching job in West Tennessee, but he discovered a "mountain of prejudice" against Annie. The problem was not racism, but sectionalism. Some Memphians felt deeply betrayed when Annie, a black southerner, left the South and relocated to the North. "Your leaving the South some time ago to live in the North brought an ill-feeling against you in some way and that's what is causing the trouble."[4] Annie sternly and confidently rejoined that she was "southern born, southern reared and when I am gone, I will be the same. I was taught the right principles of life, and principles don't change." Impressed by her confidence and optimism, Holman said she had the "right slant, and right is bound to win."[5]

Upon leaving Holman's office, a confident Annie went to nearby Brunswick, Tennessee, where she met Bert Griffin, a white community leader and grocery store owner. Annie informed him of her desire to teach in the Shelby County School

District; he agreed to help her. A few weeks later Griffin, like Squire Holman, admitted to Annie the "narrowness of human minds in high places of authority" and that some whites harbored resentment that she made "money here in the South and go to the North to spend it; then come South again to make more money to do the same again."[6] Between the world wars, white southerners displayed a certain ambivalence toward their black neighbors who exited the South. On the one hand, some were elated to pass the "negro problem" on to the North. On the other hand, others realized their need for black labor in the South. Muckraking journalist, Ray Stannard Baker, accurately expressed the dilemma of white southerners, noting, "White people were torn between their feeling of race prejudice and their downright economic needs. Hating and fearing the Negro as a race . . . they can't get along without him."[7]

Despite the lingering animosity some whites in West Tennessee harbored against her, Annie boldly and fiercely stood her ground, attesting to her honesty, "good moral character," and qualifications "to teach in the elementary schools of any county in Tennessee." Notwithstanding the opposition she encountered, Annie indeed landed a teaching job. Her thirty-dollar a month income proved to be a "great help to one who had such a little."[8]

The following semester, Annie's salary increased to sixty dollars a month when she became principal of the Cordova School. More than monetary relief, her sister provided her with mental succor. "Since I was burdened with family problems at this time," Annie testified, "my sister Emma really stuck with me to the end. In the course of time I was nursed back to better mental health by the kindness of my friends and relatives."[9] In addition to mental relief and moral support, Emma gave her an all-expense-paid trip to Miami, Florida. En route to the Sunshine State, Annie stopped in Tuskegee, Alabama, toured the Tuskegee Institute campus, and stood admiringly at the gravesite of Booker T. Washington, a "remarkable figure,"[10] who left an enduring mark on American society. She had obviously perused Washington's autobiography, and she particularly appreciated his observation that "success is to be measured not so much by the position that one has reached in life as by the obstacles which he has overcome trying to succeed."[11] Annie ingested those words and pondered them "as a lamp unto my feet and a light unto my path."[12] Annie's inspiration and optimism, then, derived not only from her faith in God and scripture, but also from her African American heroes.

While on the Tuskegee Institute campus, Tuggle dined with the renowned agriculturalist scientist, George Washington Carver. She viewed Carver as a "plain, unassuming man, but rich as cream with knowledge and understanding."[13] A former enslaved African from Missouri, Carver became an instructor at the Tuskegee Normal and Industrial Institute in 1896, after earning a master's degree in agriculture at Iowa State College of Agriculture and Mechanic Arts (later Iowa State University). As an instructor at Tuskegee, Carver helped diversify southern agriculture by devising and proposing new uses for peanuts, pecans, sweet potatoes, and other crops. Tuggle of course knew nothing of the tension and power struggle that ensued between Carver and Booker T. Washington, as scholar Linda O. McMurry has delineated;[14] Tuggle admired both men equally.

Upon departing Tuskegee, Alabama, Tuggle spent time in Atlanta, Georgia, where she worshiped with the Simpson Street Church of Christ, a congregation established by Marshall Keeble in the early 1930s. The church's minister, Sutton Johnson, had been a "star student" at the short-lived Silver Point Christian Institute (SPIC). Johnson's wife, Zeeda, prepared lunch for Tuggle before departing Atlanta. Tuggle deemed the meal a "life saver," since she had only five dollars to make it to Florida and then back to Tennessee. However, she providentially met a "very nice" Pullman porter who told her where she could find a "nice room in Miami to fit my pocketbook." The porter's friends allowed Tuggle to stay in their home for "only $1.50 for the whole three days I was there." Reflecting on the generosity of both Zeeda Johnson and the Pullman porter, Tuggle concluded, "Like Abraham of old, I could truly say God will provide."[15]

Upon arriving in Miami, Tuggle saw luscious fruit trees, the Atlantic Ocean, and the beautiful sandy beaches; consequently, the song—"Then sings my soul, My Savior God to Thee, How Great Thou Art" came to her mind. While strolling through the spacious and exquisite Biscayne Park, she contemplated the famous poem "Thanatopsis."[16] But the white grounds keeper kindly reminded Tuggle that she was not "allowed in this park. But if I were in your stead, I would take my time walking out, and view everything that came before my eyes." Tuggle called her visit "one of the greatest adventures of my life" and reflected on Acts 17:26, which states that God "hath made of one blood all nations of men for to dwell on all the face of the earth, and hath determined the times before appointed, and the bounds of their habitation." In Tuggle's view, the verse attested to the unity of humanity. The white gardener, she asserted, "realized this fact when he hated to tell a fellow human being that she was not allowed in the place that God had provided for the human family."[17] Annie Tuggle was no agitator for civil rights, but she clearly rejected racial discrimination on biblical and theological grounds.

After staying three days in Miami, Tuggle's train transported her to Jacksonville, Florida. From there, her train then returned to Atlanta, carrying her and many black Pullman porters to the Peach State for a national convention.[18] They made her welcome to all the food in their basket. One porter, sensing that Annie was "tired and worn," asked his fellow workers to "let her rest"; the men complied. Even though Tuggle's own marriage failed, she held these married men in high regard. "All the pullman porters on the train that I had just left had the marks of married men. They were so thoughtful of a poor creature like me."[19] Tuggle, despite her own failed marriage, still believed in the solemnity of matrimony because of the scriptural testimony: "It is not good that the man should be alone. (Genesis 2:18)."[20]

After returning to Memphis, Tennessee, Tuggle called her trip to Florida a "turning point in my life." It cleared her mind and was "rewarding." The hospitality and beneficence of the Pullman porters and the encounter with the white park ranger at Biscayne Park refreshed Tuggle. "I was a new person after this trip. I had new perspectives on life. It had been a most unique trip."[21]

More significantly, Tuggle overcame her own doldrums during the Great Depression by pouring her heart and soul into church work. She toiled as a "church mother" in Memphis, Tennessee. Scholar Anthea D. Butler, when assessing the contributions of African American women in the Church of God in Christ (COGIC), noted that women often acted as "advisers to the pastors, as disciplinarians and leaders of wayward church members, and as spiritual avatars to the congregation."[22] Tuggle similarly labored as a counselor, teacher, and leader in African American Churches of Christ. In 1913 black evangelist John T. Ramsey conducted a three-week gospel meeting in Memphis and called on Tuggle to read certain biblical passages during his sermons.[23] Ramsey's reliance on Tuggle attests that black ministers in Churches of Christ recognized her as a competent woman and a valuable asset to their fledgling fellowship in the early twentieth century.

Five years later, Keeble bestowed high praise on Tuggle. Keeble was in Collierville, Tennessee, to preach for two weeks, but some residents, disturbed by the evangelist's exclusivistic sermons, threatened his life. Leaders of the Collierville congregation decided to end the gospel campaign after a few nights, but Keeble urged Tuggle to talk with the church's elders and ask them to find another place for him to preach. His words startled her, rendering her speechless and almost breathless. "They would be glad to do anything you suggest," Keeble assured Tuggle, "because you have lived such a faithful life before them. They highly respect your judgment on matters of this kind because of your wonderful knowledge of the Scriptures."[24] Morally upright and biblically astute, Tuggle, in Keeble's mind, was unquestionably a woman of influence and authority.

In 1930 William H. Owens, a convert of the black preacher Alexander Campbell and a former minister in Indianapolis, Indiana, relocated to Memphis, Tennessee, and assumed oversight of the Iowa and Lauderdale Church of Christ.[25] Owens, upon learning that Tuggle possessed extensive biblical knowledge and church work experience, immediately appealed to her for spiritual assistance. "Memphis has a bright future," Owens predicted, "and I believe much good can be done here; but I need you to help me."[26] Like many other black preachers, Owens clearly understood that without the faithful and dedicated backing of black sisters like Tuggle his ministry would have been severely curtailed and ineffective. Tuggle, after pondering Owens's request, relocated from Germantown to Memphis, purchased a car, rented a small apartment near the church building, and immersed herself in the life and work of the church. Tuggle used her vehicle to help transport members back and forth to the worship services, exerted her energy and passion to canvass the black community in Memphis in search of lost souls, and used her biblical understanding to instruct Christian women. Such diligent actions caused white and black Christians in Memphis to hold Tuggle in high regard.

Tuggle's most important role as a black woman in Churches of Christ, however, was probably as a wise counselor and adviser to both men and women, blacks and whites, in her chosen religious fellowship. In 1932, for instance, white leaders from the Union Avenue Church of Christ and black members of the Iowa and Lauderdale Church of Christ convened to discuss how to strengthen and enlarge the small black congregation. Because the struggling black flock bore an eight hundred dollar debt on its building, some suggested that the preacher, William H. Owens, be terminated and that his meager salary be used to "pay what was owed on the building."[27] While Tuggle listened quietly and patiently to the conversation, her close friend, Mae Lovie Hervey, prodded her to "say something and say it now." Tuggle then stood and asserted: "Brethren, I notice that the opinion of most of the speakers is to turn the minister off and use the money on hand to pay off the debt on the building. But to my mind, when you take the gospel out of the church you have a dead church." Taking her inspiration from Romans 1:16, Tuggle insisted: "The gospel is the power of God to save." She then recommended that the leaders retain Owens as the regular minister and invite Marshall Keeble for a gospel meeting to reach out to the unsaved and "help build up the church."[28] The white and black leaders acquiesced to Tuggle's suggestion.

The 1932 meeting at the Iowa and Lauderdale Church of Christ is both instructive and significant for at least two reasons. First, African Americans and Anglos in Shelby County collaborated during an era of rigid racial separation to advance the cause of Christ. Black members of the Iowa and Lauderdale congregation readily welcomed whites from the Union Avenue Church of Christ into their business meeting because they perceptively understood that their numerical and spiritual advancement was inextricably tied to the financial support of white believers. Alexander Campbell, an African American preacher from Middle Tennessee, boldly acknowledged black Christians' dependence on white economic aid. "Dear brethren, some of the loyal colored brethren have the zeal, the whole truth, and the courage to do the right thing," Campbell testified in 1909, "and you white brethren who are loyal have the zeal, the whole truth, the courage, and the money."[29] Second, that the men of both congregations accepted and acted on Tuggle's proposal attests to her power, influence, and wisdom. An African American woman, through her temerity and sagacity, helped to guide and build up the cause of Christ in Memphis, Tennessee.

Keeble's one-month tent meeting was successful. His plain, yet powerful preaching, coupled with William Lee's melodious singing, engendered one hundred baptisms. "This was truly a great meeting," Tuggle observed. "It shook Memphis from center to circumference." She not only attributed the meeting's success to the efforts of Keeble and Lee, she further acknowledged the support of white and black Christians from Arkansas and Mississippi who helped "Memphis spread the gospel of the Son of God." William H. Owens's leadership ability, biblical knowledge, and effective debating also propelled black Churches of Christ in Memphis toward numerical and spiritual growth. Indeed, Owens, whom Tuggle deemed a man of righteousness, organized a congregation in Orange Mound, Tennessee, a suburb of Memphis and the first all-black neighborhood in the United States established by African Americans. Owens in turn recognized Tuggle's value, assigning her "to work among the sisters in the congregations there and to teach them to do their best in every way for the good of the cause of Christ."[30] Sadly several years after the impressive meeting in Memphis, Owens succumbed to an illness and died at the age of forty-five.[31] He passed away, but his work lived on in the indefatigable labor of Tuggle and in what is now the Norris Road Church of Christ.

After Owens's sudden and untimely death, G. E. Steward, a blind preacher who converted to Churches of Christ in Texas under the preaching of G. P. Bowser, became the regular minister of the Iowa and Lauderdale congregation. Steward, despite his handicap, proved to be a "God-sent man to fit in where Brother Owens left off."[32] Ella Steward, a devoted supporter of her husband's ministry, witnessed firsthand the contribution of Annie C. Tuggle to the growth of black Churches of Christ in Memphis, affirming, "The evidence of your [Tuggle's] power and influence throughout the brotherhood has not been made known by the erecting of buildings of mortar and stone as did the ancient civilizations of the world; but in sacrificing to help spread the gospel of Christ over the earth as the waters cover the sea." Steward further commended Tuggle for her "natural gift for raising funds for worthy causes in the family of God."[33]

Tuggle's ability to garner funds for worthy Christian causes captured the attention of G. P. Bowser, who in the early 1940s solicited her efforts in raising proceeds for the struggling Bowser Christian Institute in Fort Smith, Arkansas. While maintaining her residence in Memphis, Tennessee, Tuggle spent several weeks in west Arkansas, canvassing white and black congregations in Oklahoma.[34] Tuggle never disclosed whether or not her fundraising efforts were successful. Notwithstanding her silence, that Bowser looked to her as a fundraiser attests not only to her people skills but also to her competence, credibility, and influence among African American and Anglo members of Churches of Christ.

Tuggle without doubt delighted in canvassing and soliciting funds for Christian causes, but her heart was always in teaching black youth. In the early 1940s Tuggle received an invitation to teach at the Nashville Christian Institute (NCI). The brainchild of concerned black leaders and philanthropist A. M. Burton, the NCI opened its doors in 1940 to serve black youth in Churches of Christ and beyond.[35] When Tuggle arrived five years later, she filled multiple roles as secretary, dorm supervisor, and junior high teacher. Her most important role, however, remained that of mentor, counselor, and "church mother." During an annual Bible lectureship at the NCI, a young professor, after being puzzled by questions from preachers, dashed to Tuggle's classroom, pleading: "Sister Tuggle, those forty ministers got me spell bound. I'm not able to answer them. Please help me out on this question." Tuggle did not remember the question, even though the ministers were satisfied with her answer.[36]

Tuggle encountered and instructed several young men who would later emerge as prominent preachers and leaders in African American Churches of Christ. Robert Woods, a student from Gallatin, Tennessee, went on to minister for more than four decades in Chicago, Illinois. When Kelly K. Mitchell, a student from Georgia, was unprepared to give an oral presentation on "Temperance" in Tuggle's class, she upbraided him. Mitchell humbly accepted the verbal lashing and later delivered the "best presentation in the whole class." More significantly, Mitchell went on to launch a stellar preaching career in the Yellowhammer

State and beyond.[37] Tuggle's most prized students was Fred D. Gray, a native of Montgomery, Alabama. Tuggle noted that Gray was "one of the first 'boy preachers.' Fred was always obedient to me and never gave me any trouble." She was especially proud of Gray's work as a lawyer for the civil rights movement, highlighting his close association with Martin Luther King Jr., Rosa Parks, the Montgomery Bus Boycott, and the Autherine Lucy case.[38] Tuggle here displayed a social and political consciousness, a concern for the plight of American blacks across the South.

More recently, Gray acknowledged that Tuggle not only laid for him a liberal arts foundation at the NCI, but she also helped him open his first bank account, demonstrating to him the importance of good money management.[39] Tuggle furnished Gray with essential educational and practical training as a youth, yet the young Gray helped make life better for Tuggle in her later years by toppling racial barriers in the Jim Crow South. Even though the adolescent Gray may not have given Tuggle any "trouble" as an NCI student, the adult lawyer consistently made life miserable for segregationists and racists in the United States.[40]

Ever the adventurer, Tuggle worked at the NCI temporarily. In the summer of 1944, she relocated to Detroit, Michigan, where her sister and family lived. When Tuggle arrived in the Motor City, she was one of 190,000 African Americans residing there. Racial strife and economic disparity pervaded the city. The previous year, police killed seventeen black people during a devastating race riot. From 1943 to 1953, 258,614 rental units existed in Detroit; African Americans lived in 29,751 of them. Between 1940 to 1946, Motor City officials constructed 42,121 houses for white buyers, but only 860 for black purchases. African Americans consistently held such low level positions as janitors, doormen, maids, operators, and stockers in retail stores.[41]

Despite such stark social injustice and widespread racial woes, Detroit lured many black southerners because of employment opportunities in factories and industries. Additionally, the Motor City became a "mecca" for black cultural talent. Diana Ross, for instance, was born there in 1944.[42] Thirteen years later, Rosa Parks and her family moved to Detroit in search of a better life.[43] In 1959, Berry Gordy Jr. formed his own record label, Motown, and signed and produced several gifted groups such as the Supremes, the Temptations, and the Jackson Five, all of whom transformed the music industry nationally and globally.[44] This was the turbulent, yet tantalizing, Detroit that Annie Tuggle encountered in the mid-1940s.

To her surprise, W. C. Baldwin, a former classmate at the SPCI who called on Tuggle during his sermon to answer a question, had relocated to Detroit and helped her land a job at the Western Union Insurance Company in the Motor City. While working there, she acquired certain entrepreneurial skills which proved invaluable when she and her sister launched a lucrative "pie" business. Tuggle's pies were so delicious that she became known as the "Pie Lady."[45] While operating her lucrative pie business in Detroit, Tuggle found time to write and publish her first book, *Our Ministers and Song Leaders of the Church of Christ.* Published in 1945, the book contained biographical sketches of black ministers in Churches of Christ, providing insight into the life, work, and backgrounds of African American Churches of Christ in the twentieth century. The book not only attests to Tuggle's admiration of her chosen fellowship, but it also reveals her appreciation of the history of black Churches of Christ. By compiling snapshots of black preachers and song leaders in Churches of Christ, Tuggle became both a preserver and instructor of her fellowship's past.

As she had done in Memphis, Tuggle was extremely active among black Churches of Christ in Detroit. In 1946 Tuggle established the Home Training Christian Institute "for the purpose of teaching the word of God to both young and old."[46] When African Americans went north, many of them shifted their religious orientation from an otherworldly focus to a this-worldly one.[47] Hence, some Baptists in the Motor City formed both a Training School and a Children's Home, reflecting their interest in the "affairs of the community."[48] Whether Tuggle took her inspiration from Baptists or other religious groups remains unclear. Yet, it is indisputable that black women's activism, as scholar Darlene Clark Hine argues, extended beyond the church walls, encompassing "home, family and community uplift."[49]

Annie Tuggle's autobiography, *Another World Wonder,* is strangely silent on other activities that she immersed herself in while in Detroit. She never commented on the poverty and substandard housing which persisted throughout the 1950s and 1960s, sparking the Detroit race riot of 1967.[50] She did report suffering a serious car accident in 1961 that prevented her from operating her pie business effectively. Therefore, she left Detroit three years later. But perhaps Tuggle perceptively saw the handwriting on the wall and departed the Wolverine State three years before the deadly race riot. Little did she know, however, that she had returned to another environment swirling with racial strife in Memphis.

When she came back to Memphis in 1964, Tuggle worked and worshiped at the Vance Avenue Church of Christ and expressed interest in doing missionary work in the West Indies. Securing financial support from her home congregation and from other friends across the brotherhood of black Churches of Christ, Tuggle left for the Bahamas, Jamaica, and Haiti on May 5, 1967. She stayed ten days in the Bahamas with the minister, Brother Miller and his wife. Tuggle reported that Miller, a graduate of Southwestern Christian College, was an "excellent minister and preaches Christ and him crucified without addition and subtraction."[51] She then flew to Kingston, Jamaica, where A. A. Walker, a local doctor and preacher, and his wife Olive received her warmly. Dr. Walker invited Tuggle to speak to a group of nurses. "On the spur of the moment," Tuggle confessed, "I remembered a promise I made to one of my instructors while a student in Walden College—that I would do the best that was in me any time I was called on to make a speech. I did just that."[52] From Jamaica she moved on to Haiti where she stayed for three days before returning to the United States.

Tuggle's three-week visit to the West Indies proved to be life-changing, as she returned to Memphis a "new person." Her sojourn to the Bahamas, Jamaica, and Haiti prompted her to "get something started to help the millions of people on those islands. Those people were in darkness and almost without hope." She then concluded that "what was most needed was a man in the church to go to Jamaica and see first-hand the great opportunities there. Then report to the churches in America the need to go to Jamaica in large numbers to preach the gospel of the son of God to every creature under heaven without respect of race, color or previous condition."[53] The man Tuggle searched for was Woodie W. Morrison, minister of the Collegiate Heights Church of Christ in Dayton, Ohio, one of her "sons in the faith."

Morrison invited Tuggle to Ohio to speak to his congregation about her missionary trip. Seventy-eight-year-old Tuggle, standing proudly and speaking firmly as a loving church mother, stated: "Children, Jamaica is calling; the islands of the West Indies are ripe unto harvest, and we must spread the word of the Lord over those islands as the waters cover the seas, and we must do it now." After hearing her impassioned appeal, Morrison consented, affirming, "I will go" to Jamaica.[54] He took his first trip to the West Indies in the spring of 1968. Morrison later reporting, "After hearing this humble, God-fearing, battle-scarred Christian soldier speak, I knew that I had to go to Jamaica and see what the Lord wanted Collegiate Heights to do in the area of missions in Jamaica."[55]

Tuggle's impassioned appeal before black Christians in Ohio confirms that she was not only committed to spreading the gospel beyond the borders of the United States, but that she was truly a church mother with influence; her demeanor and words could sway men and women and move people in a positive direction. Even though Tuggle lived in Memphis from 1964 to 1971, a period when that city witnessed widespread racial violence including the death of Martin Luther King Jr., her heart was clearly focused on matters beyond the racial tension of Shelby County. Like many others in African American Churches of Christ, Tuggle was seemingly preoccupied with addressing the spiritual needs of black people and not their racial, social, and economic concerns. Upon returning from the West Indies, she expressed, "My heart's desire and prayer will ever be to Him for help to unshackle and expand my soul to the fullest realization of His wonders and blessings towards human beings."[56] For Tuggle, unshackling one's soul and embracing the Lord's spiritual blessings superseded any interest in social or economic justice.

In essence, Tuggle's failed marriage and her lack of children proved to be a blessing in disguise for it freed her to cast her energy wholly into the work of the church and permitted her to travel extensively. Even though she had no biological children of her own, she poured her life into the young men and women whom she encountered at the NCI and elsewhere. Many of her spiritual progeny became principal leaders in African American Churches of Christ such as Fred D. Gray, Kelly K. Mitchell, and Robert Woods. She regarded black ministers A. A. Walker and Woodie Morrison as "my two sons in the faith."[57] Tuggle defied traditional roles in Churches of Christ by reading scripture in public, by speaking out in business meetings, and by advising church leaders regarding spiritual matters. In this regard, Tuggle assumed leadership roles even when some men and women in her chosen fellowship deemed such action inappropriate.

PART III

THE BURDEN OF RELIGION

1969–1976

Presentation of a portrait of Annie C. Tuggle, February 1976.
From left: Lena Carr, Annie C. Tuggle, Carroll Pitts, Mark Carr, and Bernice Pitts.

CHAPTER 5

"BUT YOU CAN'T WHIP THIS BIBLE"

The Burden of Scripture

"And that from a child thou hast known the holy scriptures, which are able to make thee wise unto salvation through faith which is in Christ Jesus."

—2 TIMOTHY 3:15

The story of scripture provided Annie C. Tuggle with a moral compass and a source of spiritual formation, profoundly shaping her heart and soul. Upon learning that her mother, Mollie, had prayed fervently for Annie while she still lay in her womb, Tuggle immediately linked her mother's piety with the biblical character Hannah. "I remembered reading in the Bible about Hannah and how she prayed to God for a man child and God answered her prayer."[1] Annie never forgot her mother's pious act and always recalled the Old Testament narrative which molded her own life and helped engender her faith in the God of scripture. "From a close study of the Bible I have found over the years that it gives 'all things pertaining to life and godliness.'

When a person does not know, it is best to listen to [J]eremiah, who said, 'Thus saith the Lord; Stand ye in the ways, and seek, and ask for the old paths, wherein is the good way, and walk therein and ye shall find rest for your soul. (Jeremiah 6:16).'"[2] For Tuggle, the Bible remained an all-sufficient and life-giving burden.

African Americans dealt with scripture on several levels. Enslaved Africans had viewed the Bible as "the Talking Book" with power, convinced that it possessed the potency to transform their lives and their circumstances.[3] Under the impulses and influences of the first Second Great Awakening, African Americans learned to interpret scripture freely and eclectically, accepting parts of it, while rejecting other segments. Free blacks in the North read the Bible to champion social equality and a civil rights agenda, adopting Galatians 3:28 as their pivotal text. Later, the African American sects which flourished in the late nineteenth and early twentieth centuries espoused a "fundamental disdain for and mistrust of American society."[4] Finally, even though not directly influenced by the fundamentalist movement in North America, many black Christians read the Bible without regard for the "historical experiences of persons of African descent in this country."[5]

Annie Tuggle clearly drew from this matrix of black biblical interpretation in shaping her own biblical perceptions. "The Bible was indispensable for me," she averred. "It was my all and all. . . . Whatever my work was, around the house, I made preparation to place my Bible where I could look into it when different portions of Scripture came to my mind and I was not sure just how it read."[6] Tuggle appropriated the Bible in three fundamental ways: She read it to champion the cause of human equality; she studied it through the lens of Campbellian rationalism; she personalized and used it as her moral guide.

Even though not a civil rights activist, Tuggle boldly and creatively brought scripture into her argument for human equality. When she visited the beautiful Biscayne Park in Miami, Florida, the white supervisor reluctantly told Tuggle she must leave because of the park's Deep South segregationist policies. Tuggle, while slowly exiting the magnificent garden, noted that "This was one of the greatest adventures of my life because I was shown of a certainty that God hath made of one blood all nations of men for to dwell on all the face of the earth, and hath determined the times before appointed and the bounds of their habitation. (Acts 17:26)."[7]

Tuggle again highlighted the significance of the same passage in reflecting on her relationship with a white woman she befriended in Memphis. Tuggle's white neighbor, married with two small children, confided in her that rumors circulated that her husband was unfaithful to her. Tuggle counseled her that as long as her husband cared for her and their children and brought home his entire paycheck, the gossip was meaningless and the "work of Satan." However, after the woman discovered that her husband was indeed cheating on her, she vowed to kill both her husband and his lover. Tuggle, who had recently gone through a divorce, displayed empathy: "I went to her then, put my arms around her, kissed her and told her that she meant everything to her children and to me." "I am going to do all I can to help you," she added sympathetically. "I stayed a long time in her home that evening, but not in her presence." The next day, the betrayed woman thanked Tuggle for consolation and confessed: "Annie, I owe you more than I will ever be able to pay. You have saved me from doing that awful deed. I am so glad that you encouraged me not to ruin myself for life with something that is worthless."[8]

Although Tuggle never divulged the aftermath of her neighbor's betrayal, she used the incident to argue for human equality. "Blood is thicker than water," she maintained. Citing Acts 17:26, Tuggle added that "the Bible teaches, God has made of one blood all nations to dwell on the earth. Our souls were knit together in love as that of David and Jonathan found in 1 Samuel 18:1, because we both were a part of the same human family."[9] That a black woman counseled and bonded emotionally with a distraught white woman in the segregated South is strikingly significant.

Certainly Tuggle's appropriation of Acts 17:26 was not unique. After white police officers in Winona, Mississippi, savagely beat Fannie Lou Hamer, she had a conversation with the jailer's wife who showed kindness to Hamer and the other prisoners by giving them cold water. Hamer asked the jailer's wife to open her Bible and read Proverbs 26:26 and Acts 17:26. "The New Testament passage came from St. Paul's address to the Athenians at Mars Hill," explained Hamer. "Before a people who took great pride in its collective piety—in this respect, a people much like the Mississippi faithful white churchgoers." She particularly stressed Acts 17:26, "God hath made of one blood all nations of men for to dwell on all the face of the earth," which she interpreted to mean that "all races are one in

God's sight." The jailer's wife wrote down the verses, but she never returned.[10]

Yet Tuggle's use of scripture was unique because she was a black adherent of a Restorationist fellowship, an affiliation which deeply affected how she interpreted scripture. Her brother-in-law, Joe Holmes, had introduced the Bible to her "as the revealed will of God to man." When addressing the subject of baptism, Holmes stressed to Tuggle the seminal prepositional phrase "for the remission of sins" in Acts 2:38.[11] He further emphasized James 1:27 to show that "Religion is a duty to perform." African Americans in Churches of Christ, like their white counterparts, opposed the Calvinistic tenets of predestination and total depravity of the human will and espoused a rigid brand of Arminianism. Tuggle's other chief black biblical instructors included her sister, Gertrude Holmes, and ministers, Henry Garrett and Robert Burton—all of whom helped lead her from Methodism into Churches of Christ.[12]

White leaders in Churches of Christ, however, exerted their influence on Tuggle's black instructors. Over the five-decade period, from 1866 to 1917, David Lipscomb, through the pages of the *Gospel Advocate*, left an indelible mark on the biblical understanding of African American Churches of Christ.[13] Lipscomb held up the Bible as a "book of law which every Christian act must be 'authorized.'" He further advocated a Campbellian division of scripture, insisting that for Christians the New Testament was authoritative over the Old Testament.[14] More specifically, Tuggle came under the influence of N. B. Hardeman, a leading white evangelist. While a student at Walden College in Nashville,

Tuggle attended the noted Hardeman Tabernacle sermons which the white preacher delivered on five different occasions in the Music City between 1922 and 1942. She recalled "hearing every sermon Bro. Hardeman preached in the Rymon [*sic*] Auditorium in Nashville. As a young lady, these sermons had a tremendous impact upon my life."[15] These discourses not only exerted tremendous influence on white ministers and members in Churches of Christ,[16] but they also molded the theological outlook of blacks in that fellowship.

From Hardeman, Tuggle acquired a hardening exclusivistic and combative theological posture. His sermon, "Why a Member of the Church of Christ?" especially affected her, as he highlighted the authority of the Bible, rejecting human leaders as not God ordained. Hardeman asserted, "The man who is right before God respects the Bible first of all, while business secular, and material considerations are wholly secondary." When contrasting the Churches of Christ with other religious entities, he affirmed, "If I build, ladies and gentlemen, upon Swedenborg, Buddha, Confucius, Luther, Knox, Calvin, Wesley, Campbell, Joe Smith Jr., Mrs. Eddy, or any other human being, I am but building upon the sand, and God said that the man who so does will ultimately and at last see his house collapse."[17] Tuggle marked the Hardeman campaign as of "great historical importance" which was "felt . . . throughout this whole country of ours," and she hailed the preacher "a man of God."[18] She later praised Hardeman as a naturally gifted speaker with "a sonorous, melodious voice; strengthened by the impression of power and immeasurable reserve force," who, despite his natural ability, relied on the power of God's Spirit to engender faith in his listeners. Tuggle concluded, "Well may it be said of the sermons delivered by Brother Hardeman during the series of meetings that they were 'very seasonable, very reasonable, and very eloquent.'"[19]

When converting from Methodism to Churches of Christ in 1908, Tuggle's mother, Mollie, chided her for not getting permission from her father and the Methodist Church officials to leave. Referring to Matthew 10:37, Annie insisted that her allegiance to Christ superseded all family and religious ties. She maintained that "as for the Methodist Church, it's the devil's work and I don't have to get permission from the devil to obey Christ!"[20] The following year Mollie also became a member of Churches of Christ under the preaching of G. P. Bowser. Annie's reputation as a knowledgeable student of scripture permeated the Germantown community, but her close relative Ellen Reed, a devout Methodist, determined to expose Annie. "Ann, I came up here to whip you," Reed barked. "Everybody is talking about how you can make all these people around here shut their mouths when it comes to talking about religion. I was reading the Bible long before you were born. I'm here to whip you once for always this day." Annie, contemplating the advice in James 1:19 to think before speaking, replied meekly yet firmly: "Cousin Sis, it would be an easy thing to whip me because I am nothing to start with, but you can't whip this Bible." She then alluded to Matthew 24:35, which attested to the permanence of scripture, and added, "Christ said heaven and earth will pass away but my word will not pass away and his word is what I have to offer you, so you may start now to whip the word of God and not me."[21]

Tuggle's firm words profoundly impacted her older cousin; after daily studying with her cousin, Reed became convinced that she needed to be baptized into Churches of Christ. Reed asked Tuggle to baptize her in a pond near her house, but Annie refused, lamenting, "I would be glad to but I am a woman and it is not Scriptural for a woman to baptize as taught in the Bible." She then recommended that Reed attend church services on Sunday and seek baptism from a church leader. Tuggle rejoiced when her older relative was "baptized into Christ and became a new creature."[22]

The story of Ellen Reed's transition into Churches of Christ reveals Tuggle's exclusivistic theological posture and combative demeanor which seemed at odds with her obvious humility, revealing what historian Forrest G. Wood has called "the arrogance of faith." For Tuggle, then, the Bible was both a weapon to confront what she viewed as religious error as well as a burden which she struggled to shoulder. Tuggle's refusal to comply with Reed's request to baptize her laid bare the tension in her heart; she desired to provide Reed with spiritual direction, while her understanding of the Bible forbade her from baptizing her cousin. This was the paradoxical burden of scripture which Tuggle bore.[23]

That Tuggle espoused a militant attitude toward other religious groups and viewed scripture as a weapon against religious error emerges in her dialogue with another cousin, Annie B. Tuggle. Annie C. considered Annie B. "very intelligent but a member of the Methodist Church." Annie B. was confident the "Methodist Church and its doctrine were right" because John Wesley was Methodism's founder. Annie C. visited Annie B.'s house to show her that "the Bible is the New Testament of our Lord and Saviour Jesus Christ. John Wesley is not in it and no other men who have started churches of their own." Annie C. convinced her cousin that "the Bible is right" and she too became a member of Churches of Christ.[24] Annie C. Tuggle's understanding of and respect for the "silence of Scripture" convinced her that her religious community was biblically right while all others were wrong.

For herself, Annie C. Tuggle personalized scripture, finding in it her moral compass. She read her personal experiences into the Bible and she applied it to her encounters with others throughout her life. When her aunt Sophia prepared Annie's lunch to take to LeMoyne Normal Institute because "she did not want me to be hungry," Tuggle instantly "thought of Christ when he told his disciples that he had meat to eat that they knew not of." She then appropriated John 4:34, "My meat is to do the will of him that sent me, and to finish his work," as inspiration to equip herself "to help spread the word of the Lord over the earth as the waters cover the sea."[25]

On another occasion Tuggle borrowed Aunt Sophia's expensive coat without permission to wear to a LeMoyne–Lane baseball game. Upon seeing her aunt sitting on the front porch as she returned from the ball game, Tuggle quickly tossed the costly garment "in some weeds" and dashed into the house "waving my hand as I passed her on the porch," blaming her haste on the baseball game. Later that night Tuggle went outside and retrieved Aunt Sophia's coat and exclaimed that "Everything worked out in my favor and I was reminded of Paul's statement when he said: 'All things work together for good to them that love God, to them that are called according to his purpose' [Romans 8:28]."[26] Tuggle saw the hand of God in all events, even those involving some chicanery.

At the age of nineteen, Tuggle had become the principal of the 115 pupil, all-black Promised Land School in Millington, Tennessee. Dr. Chambus, the school's director, sternly admonished her to live a morally clean life. "My knowledge of the Bible really helped me in this case," reflected Tuggle. "Immediately I thought of Joseph and how young he was when he was sold into Egypt and yet God was with him. I remembered Daniel and the three Hebrew children and how God was with them, so I was comforted by just remembering that God cares for his own."[27] Even though Tuggle was a "New Testament Christian,"[28] Old Testament narratives helped mold and shape her character.

In 1918 Marshall Keeble, the emerging black evangelist, came to Collierville, Tennessee, to conduct a two-week meeting. The campaign ended abruptly, however, after "ruffians began to cut the tent and do other mischievous things." Keeble approached Tuggle and asked her to confer with the elders of a nearby white congregation to help him continue the evangelistic effort in another location. A puzzled Tuggle doubted whether white church officials would take her suggestions seriously because of her race and gender. Reluctantly acting on what she called "the heavenly vision," a reference to St. Paul's statement in Acts 26:19, Tuggle met with the church leaders, asserting: "Brethren, you have made preparation for a two-weeks' meeting and you should not let the devil overthrow you. When the apostle Paul and

Barnabas met a case like this, they waxed bold and said, 'Seeing that ye judge yourselves unworthy of eternal life, lo we turn to the Gentiles.' (Acts 13:46)." She then cited the Great Commission in Matthew 28:18–20 and explained to the elders, "You have the 'go' sign from Christ and the gospel preacher is here and ready and willing to go." The elders, prompted by Tuggle's vigorous counsel, quickly set up a tent in Hilltop, a subdivision in Whitehaven, Tennessee, where Keeble continued his preaching campaign.[29]

The conditions at Hilltop, according to Tuggle, proved worse than at Collierville, as many neighbors "brought guns under the tent where everyone could see them, and threatened Bro. Keeble's life if he said their mother's religion was not acceptable to God." Impressed by Marshall Keeble's courage, humility, and wisdom and convinced that God would preserve the black evangelist's life, Tuggle found comfort in two biblical passages. "I honestly believed that if our spiritual eyes could have been opened as the eyes of Elisha's servant, Gehazi, we could have seen the streets of Hilltop filled with horses and chariots of fire around and about Bro. Keeble for protection. Like the apostle, Bro. Keeble determined to know nothing among them but Jesus Christ and Him crucified."[30]

Old Testament teachings had also buoyed Tuggle in the difficulties she encountered during her Middle Tennessee sojourn. After the Silver Point Christian Institute (SPCI) closed, Tuggle returned home and related the deplorable situation to her mother who surprisingly offered over twenty acres of land, provided the school relocated to West Tennessee. Startled by her mother's generosity, Tuggle exclaimed, "I had no idea that she thought in terms like that! In my daydreams and visions, I could see a ladder as did Jacob on his way to Haran set up on the earth and the top of it reached to heaven and angels of God ascending and descending to direct the steps of these two friends."[31] Even though her mother's proposal never came to fruition, Tuggle believed that the same God who directed Jacob's uncertain future guided her and her mother as well.

Tuggle's faith in God and scripture derived in part from her mother, who compared herself to the Old Testament character Job. "Yes, God's word will stand forever and I am willing to trust him," Mollie Tuggle declared. Fusing biblical references from Proverbs 27:1, Job 13:15, and Hebrews 11:10, she continued: "We never know what a day will bring forth and I am like Job of old when he said 'though he slay me yet will I trust him.' I have had many hardships since Brother Bowser baptized me into Christ, but I am still working for that city which hath foundations whose builder and maker is God."[32] Like her mother Mollie, Annie at times compared herself to biblical characters. In 1913 P. H. Black and his wife cordially welcomed her into their Nashville home before she moved on to Silver Point, Tennessee. "They greeted me as though the apostle Paul had commended me unto them as he commended Phoebe unto the church at Rome."[33]

Three decades later when Tuggle began her brief teaching career at the Nashville Christian Institute (NCI) in 1943, the dilapidated building, insufficient teaching equipment, and lack of Christian teachers appalled her. "I was like the prophet Jeremiah," she lamented, "when he saw the condition of his people in Israel in the long ago and said, 'Oh, that my head were waters, and mine eyes a fountain or tears that I might weep day and night for the slain daughters of my people.' (Jer. 9:1)."[34] By linking her personal experiences with biblical characters, Tuggle merely expanded on a long and sacred tradition of black interpretation of scripture. Jarene Lee, a Methodist preacher whom Richard Allen ordained, recounted her conversion experience, testifying, "I trembled like *Belshazzar*, and cried out in the horror of my spirit, 'God be merciful to me a sinner.'"[35]

In addition to applying scripture to her own life, Tuggle connected biblical characters and verses with those she met. While enrolled at the SPCI, discord ensued between Tuggle and another student, "just as it came up between Abraham's servants and Lot's servants." Thankfully G. P. Bowser intervened and solved the dispute.[36] When soliciting funds for the SPCI, Tuggle had visited the home of David Lipscomb, one of her fellowship's pivotal figures. Initially unsure whether to allow Tuggle to confer with the aging patriarch "in his declining years physically,"[37] Mrs. Lipscomb consented after seeing her grave demeanor and determination. Mr. Lipscomb confessed to Tuggle that although he had no money, he vowed to use his "influence to see that you have an institution where the Bible can be taught daily as a textbook to the students. Leaving the Lipscomb home, Tuggle felt that she "had talked with an angel direct from heaven." "Bro. Lipscomb was a true servant of God," she added, "and that's all the angel could have been." She then cited part of Proverbs 18:24, "He that would have friends first must show himself friendly," and applied it to the Lipscomb couple. "Bro. and Sister Lipscomb did just that to me and I can never forget them."[38]

In the summer of 1923, Tuggle worked as a maid in A. M. Burton's Life and Casualty Company building as well as in his home, earning fourteen dollars weekly. The Burton's home, set "among the seven hills in the city of Nashville," reminded Tuggle "of the story of Rome when she sat on her seven hills of beauty and ruled the world. Both Brother and Sister Burton were great, but they did not try to rule the world." The humility and hospitality of the wealthy Burtons pointed people to the Ultimate Ruler of the universe as "they helped many people to know the true and living God who ruleth in the kingdom of men and giveth it to whomsoever he wills. (Daniel 4:32)."[39]

Tuggle drew on her deep familiarity with the book of Jeremiah when she compared William H. Owens, minister of the Iowa and Lauderdale Church of Christ in Memphis, to a prophet, lauding him as "one like Jeremiah described (Jer. 5:1), 'a man that executeth judgment and seeketh the truth.'" Owens's leadership strengths, Tuggle elaborated, included "his knowledge of people and the know-how to deal with them. He never tried to drive them, but encouraged and influenced them to do according to thus saith the Lord."[40] She linked one of her own most accomplished NCI students, Fred Gray, to a lawyer mentioned in the Book of Titus. "If Paul were alive today, perhaps he would say, 'Bring Fred Gray the lawyer, as he said, 'Bring Ze[n]as the lawyer in Titus 3:13."[41]

Annie C. Tuggle was a dedicated student of scripture even if she was not a biblical scholar. She was not trained in Hebrew, Aramaic, or Koine Greek, yet the Bible saturated her mind, profoundly shaping her thinking and molding her character. For her, scripture was both a blessing and a kindly burden. It blessed her by furnishing her spiritual comfort in times of distress and moral guidance in times of uncertainty. Like countless other African Americans, Tuggle read scripture to support the cause of racial and social equality. But she also read her Bible through Campbellian rationalism, which inspired her rigidly exclusivistic theological posture as she submitted to its mandates in a theologically rigid and exclusivistic fellowship. Despite this myopia, the Bible also furnished Tuggle with an unshakable faith and a sturdy spiritual foundation. "There is nothing impossible with him who puts his faith in God and keeps trying," she declared. "The great Apostle Paul once said: 'I can do all things through Christ who strengtheneth [*sic*] me.' In our efforts to serve our heavenly Father by contributing to human welfare and human happiness, we may march against a barbed wire fence, but let us push forward to the last notch; fight the battles to the better end [*sic*]."[42] Tuggle not only believed those words; she practiced them in her lifelong effort to serve God by "contributing to human welfare and human happiness."

CHAPTER 6

"THE STORY OF MY LIFE"

Another World Wonder

by Annie C. Tuggle

"I, on my side, require of every writer, first or last, a simple and sincere account of his own life."

–HENRY DAVID THOREAU

In 1971 Annie C. Tuggle left Memphis, Tennessee, and came to live in Perris, California. Her two nephews, George F. Johnson and Albert H. Johnson, who had relocated earlier to California, persuaded Tuggle to join almost one and a half million African American residents. Tuggle immediately found her church home at the West Seventh Church of Christ, an integrated congregation. While in Southern California, Tuggle met several black members and leaders in African American Churches of Christ in the Los Angeles area. More importantly, two years later Tuggle, at age eighty-three, wrote and published her intriguing autobiography, *Another World Wonder*, a book strikingly similar to those of other black women who told their stories of triumph over the twin evils of chattel enslavement and legalized segregation.[1]

Annie C. Tuggle's *Another World Wonder* parallels in some ways Mary Church Terrell's *A Colored Woman in a White World.* Like Tuggle, Terrell was a native of Shelby County, Tennessee, and a daughter of formerly enslaved Africans. After earning her degree at Oberlin College in Ohio, Terrell taught classical languages in Wilberforce, Ohio, and later Washington, DC. Because of her presence and position in the nation's capital, she conferred with Theodore Roosevelt's cabinet members in the wake of the infamous 1906 Brownsville incident, hoping to suspend the dishonorable discharge sentences for the unjustly prosecuted African American soldiers. Even though Tuggle enjoyed no such access to political leaders and was not as widely renowned or as broadly traveled as Terrell, Tuggle seems to have carefully read Terrell's autobiography first published in 1940. The topics of race and gender permeated Terrell's work. "A white woman has only one handicap to overcome—that of sex," Terrell lamented. "I have two—both sex and race. I belong to the only group in this country which has two such huge obstacles to surmount."[2]

For Tuggle, however, a trio of issues—race, gender, and religion—pervaded her autobiography. Her painstakingly chronicled encounters with racism and sexism across the segregated South, her spiritual pilgrimage from Methodism into Churches of Christ, and her struggles as an educated black woman in a male-dominated religious fellowship make Tuggle's story unique as both an autobiography and a history of twentieth-century African American Churches of Christ. In the "Acknowledgement" section of *Another World Wonder,* she notes that many people encouraged her to "write the story of my life,"[3] yet Tuggle understood that in rehearsing her own story she was simultaneously telling the stories of countless other silent black women. Even though her gender prevented her from occupying an official leadership role in Churches of Christ, her work as a chronicler and historian placed her in a prominent and visible position, imposing a special responsibility.

Tuggle's title, *Another World Wonder,* expresses her constant wonder and surprise at God's presence and activity in her life. The title sprang not from arrogance and pride but from a humility that marveled at why God used her to do so many things well beyond her own power or talent. This seemed to Tuggle "another world wonder." Carroll Pitts, a prominent black preacher in Churches of Christ and a close friend of Tuggle, commented that she chose the title "primarily because it is almost unbelievable the way God has used her life in the church these past 83 years, and because so many people across the years have asked her to write the story of her unusual life."[4]

The themes of wonder, amazement, excitement, and surprise permeate *Another World Wonder*. C. M. Callis, a white grocery store owner in Germantown, Tennessee, allowed fourteen-year-old Annie to buy food on credit only "because he knew my family." When Tuggle visited the store later, the store manager chided her for not paying for her grocery bill. Thankful that she had learned early in life to "always get a receipt when you pay your bills," she explained: "Yes, sir, Mr. Callis, it was ten dollars in small change, and I counted it out to you, you thanked me and put it in your cash drawer." Even though the proprietor could find no record of Tuggle's payment, he accepted her word and marked "the account paid." "This took place 78 years ago," Tuggle wrote, "and still I am greatly shocked by even thinking over it. I wonder and wonder how Mr. Callis could take my word against his book. How could he put that much confidence in a teenager who had nothing to offer?" She added, "And now, another World Wonder! The greatest of all is: Why do so many of my friends and fellow workers in the church desire the story of my life in book form? I wonder, I wonder, I wonder!!"[5]

When contemplating her mother's prayers for her before she was born, her stable family background, her conversion from Methodism to Churches of Christ, her leading several of her family members into her newly-discovered fellowship, and her appointment as leader of an all-female congregation in Germantown, Tuggle again expressed astonishment over God's working in her young life. "As I reflect back more than eight decades ago and consider the experiences of my early childhood years, I really wonder how it all happened. To me, it is another World Wonder!"[6]

In the spring of 1910, Tuggle appeared at the LeMoyne Normal Institute to take the Shelby County teachers' examination. While there, she met "many of the great teachers of Shelby County and of the City of Memphis," especially G. P. Hamilton, principal of Kortrecht High School, city's only advanced school for African Americans. Obviously stunned by Tuggle's beauty and charisma, Hamilton named her "the 'Belle' of the Institute and that was my name the whole time I was there. It is a mystery to me just why he named me that and I'm afraid I shall never know. To me it is another world wonder."[7] Tuggle may well have read

Hamilton's *The Bright Side of Memphis* which highlighted the economic and educational achievements of black Memphians; this book might have inspired her to recount later in *Another World Wonder* the struggles and successes of African American Churches of Christ.

In the fall of 1925, Tuggle received an appointment as principal of the Hamner Taylor School in Memphis. After securing the position she confessed that "My heart was bubbling over with thanksgiving to God for his love and kindness toward me—a person of low estate." A well-known photographer frequently visited her school to find a proper time to take pictures of the faculty and students. The "tall, well built and eloquent" photographer came to the school several weeks later, took photographs, returned them "neatly finished," and confronted the principal, stating: "Miss Tuggle, if you were a white girl I would ask you to marry me, because you suit me in every way and I would be pleased to spend the rest of my life with you as man and wife. If you were white, there is but one thing to keep you from being my wife and that is you would have to tell me point blank 'I do not want you for a husband.'" Tuggle left the photographer, apparently a white man, unnamed. He never returned to the school, but Tuggle was so taken aback by the man's quasi-proposal that "The only thing that I can say after the elapse of 47 years is 'Another World Wonder.'"[8]

In 1967 Tuggle, like many African Americans in Churches of Christ, lamented the closing of the Nashville Christian Institute (NCI). She reprinted the *Gospel Advocate*'s announcement of the school's demise in *Another World Wonder*. Despite her deep disappointment, Tuggle correctly noted, "With the closing of N.C.I., an important era in Christian Education for Negro Christian came to a close." She also stood amazed that during the school's tenure, the Lord had worked through her to transform young lives while there. "It is 'Another World Wonder' to me that God had used me in a small way in this chapter of development in the history of my people."[9]

Tuggle also saw God's hand in her life between 1944 and 1964, when she lived in Detroit working as an insurance agent, a "pie lady," and director of a Christian Home. In 1945 she published her first book, *Our Ministers and Song Leaders of the Church of Christ*, a collection of biographical sketches of black preachers and song directors in African American Churches of Christ. During this two-decade period, Tuggle developed a number of enduring relationships. "These [friends] encouraged me and helped me to be used by God in the printing of 'Our Preachers and Song Leaders', the printing and distribution of religious tracts, the establishment of a Christian School and operating a successful business. The thought came, Another World Wonder!"[10]

After she returned to Tennessee in the mid 1960s, H. P. Knipmeyers, a representative for the Missouri Pacific Railroad Company, rang Tuggle's doorbell and explained to her that the federal government had launched an expansion program that required "practically all" of the Memphis subdivision where she lived. Knipmeyers offered her ten thousand dollars for the property. Tuggle then met with Tom Price, a railroad company lawyer, who was impressed that she had such a clear mind and good understanding for an eighty-year-old woman. Tuggle recorded, "I do not remember what I said to him, but now the only thing that is left for me to say is, 'Another World Wonder.'"[11] Price later informed Tuggle that there was a discrepancy in the property record, but she refused to worry about the situation after the "words of the prophet Daniel came ringing in my ears 'That the most High ruleth in the kingdom of men.'"[12] Shortly thereafter Tuggle sold her property for $10,500.

For Tuggle, her life's story was larger than a mere personal narrative. Consumed with a desire to connect others with God through her autobiography, she devoted the funds generated from the book's sale to help disseminate the gospel of Jesus. "Now that I have a monthly Social Security check, I want all proceeds from this book, after all expenses, to go to spreading the gospel over the earth as the waters cover the sea. When it does, this, too, will be another world wonder!"[13]

Reflecting her commitment to God and Scripture, Tuggle laced the preface of *Another World Wonder* with scriptural citations, weaving together James 1:17, 1 Peter 1:4, 2 Timothy 2:15, Isaiah 62:10. The preface further reveals the impetus of Tuggle's life and ministry, namely, to know and do "what is pleasing in the sight of the Father of lights with whom is no variableness neither shadow of turning."[14]

The body of *Another World Wonder*, however, remains unique and significant for a number of important reasons. First, Tuggle's autobiography proffers a singular glimpse into a strong black family in the Jim Crow South. Very few African Americans could chronicle their family's history and background as thoroughly and meticulously as did Tuggle. Although living in a rigidly segregated society, Tuggle and her eight siblings grew up in a devout and industrious family. They worked their own land, grew their own crops, and raised their own livestock, becoming a self-sustaining and self-affirming family in the post–Civil War South. The Tuggles, through grit and grace, faith and fortitude, survived and flourished in a viciously racist society which placed every possible obstacle in such a family's path. Indeed, they represent in microcosm, countless African American families, who though profoundly affected by chattel enslavement, bested it and its "not-too-distant-cousin-of-slavery,"[15] de jure segregation buttressed by implacable lynch law.

Refusing to be isolated by segregation, however, Tuggle also knew and interacted with pivotal white members and ministers in Churches of Christ. *Another World Wonder*, then, was a text with bi-racial, bi-gender, and Mason-Dixon Line–blurring text. Tuggle admired and esteemed principal white leaders such as David Lipscomb, A. M. Burton, H. Leo Boles, B. C. Goodpasture, and N. B. Hardeman, yet she also venerated and collaborated with such noteworthy black preachers as G. P. Bowser, Marshall Keeble, Levi Kennedy, and G. E. Steward, among others. *Another World Wonder* highlighted as well Tuggle's encounters with Margaret Lipscomb, Lillie Burton, Effie White, and the Shappley sisters. Aside from her immediate family members, Millie Black, Fannie R. Bowser, and Ella Steward, all dedicated black women in Churches of Christ, greatly inspired and impacted Tuggle's life. "As I look back over 65 years as a member of the church of Christ," she reflected, "I can see that my life, my faithfulness and my work in the church of Christ, were all deeply influenced by black and white church leaders. These great men included preachers, elders, teachers, editors, businessmen and even godly women."[16]

With an appreciative bow to the history of her faith tradition, *Another World Wonder* looks backward to black pioneer preachers who laid the foundation for African American Churches of Christ during its fledgling existence. Black trailblazers included Alexander Campbell, P. H. Black, Henry Clay, Nathaniel Cathey, and J. Tom Daniel, among others. Campbell, after severing ties with Preston Taylor and other black Disciples of Christ congregations in Nashville, Tennessee, launched the "mother church," the Jackson Street Church of Christ, among African Americans there.[17] Tuggle first met Black and his wife, Millie, in 1913 when she was transitioning from LeMoyne Normal Institute to the Silver Point Christian Institute. Henry Clay, a Civil War veteran, gave spiritual and financial assistance to G. P. Bowser's struggling Silver Point Christian Institute.[18] Nathaniel and Frances Cathey, committed Christians from Arkansas, were the grandparents of R. N. Hogan, a fervent critic of racism in white Churches of Christ and their schools.[19] J. Tom Daniel, a Middle Tennessee native, was among the first black preachers in Churches of Christ to transport the "pure gospel" to Chicago, Illinois.[20] Tuggle attempted to pay due honor to such past paladins.

Another World Wonder also looked forward in highlighting the talent of promising black youth in Churches of Christ. Tuggle understood the vital importance of the training of young people for the future growth and expansion of African American

Churches of Christ. She taught at the Nashville Christian Institute when Kelly K. Mitchell, a future preacher in Montgomery, Robert Woods, a future minister in Chicago, and Fred Gray, a future attorney for the civil rights movement, studied there.[21] Tuggle lived and worked in Detroit, where in 1951 Orum Trone Sr. launched the National Youth Conference for African American Churches of Christ. These annual gatherings afforded black youths in Churches of Christ an opportunity to interact with each other and "to participate in a spiritual feast of speeches, choral singing, prayer and wholesome Christian fellowship."[22]

Even though Tuggle grew up in West Tennessee, her spiritual commitment compelled her to traverse the nation, south and north, east and west. Her quest for a Christian education with the Bible at the center led her to the Silver Point Christian Institute in Middle Tennessee. Her associations with Christians in the Volunteer State then led her northward, as she visited such African American Christians as J. Tom Daniel and his wife who joined the waves of black immigrants flocking to the "Promised Land" of Chicago.[23] Tuggle's marriage to Dr. John Waller led her to Ohio where she enjoyed economic success, but her marriage failed. So she returned to West Tennessee for several years before relocating with her sister, Irene, to Detroit, living there from 1944 to 1964. Tuggle came back to Memphis in 1964 and remained in the city until 1971. While living in the River City, Tuggle constantly worked for the Lord, as her connections and evangelistic zeal carried her briefly to the West Indies. Tuggle, while an adventurer and a globetrotter, had evolved from a provincial black woman reared in a small Tennessee town to a Christian advocate whose compassion for others spilled over beyond the borders of the United States.

Annie Tuggle's interest in others also reached beyond her personal church affiliation. While she adhered to a narrow theology of religious fellowship, she eagerly sought, appreciated, and learned from a widening body of acquaintances, insofar as allowed by the straightened societal rules which racism so strictly enforced. In *Another World Wonder,* she tells of meeting, through her brother Dewey, with Willis Weatherly, a graduate student at the University of Cincinnati, who impressed Tuggle as a wise and insightful young man.[24] After matriculating at LeMoyne Normal Institute in Memphis, Tuggle encountered Ludwig T. Larsen, the school's principal, and a seemingly "very fine gentleman."[25] Jeroy Meacham, a tall, dark-skinned student at Lane College and "as polite as a basket of chips," invited her to a social hour. Meacham later became a physician in Madison County, Tennessee.[26] Tuggle called the president of Lane College, J. F. Lane, "one of the finest persons I have ever met."[27]

While preparing to take the state's examination for teachers, Tuggle felt honored that she had met G. P. Hamilton, the influential educator of black city schools in Memphis.[28] She lauded the extraordinary achievements of George W. Gore Jr., her former English teacher at Tennessee A & I State University, and who, after earning advanced degrees from Columbia and Harvard Universities, was appointed the first African American member of the National Education Association.[29] Tuggle's dining with the remarkable agricultural scientist, George Washington Carver, proved to be an unforgettable experience.[30] Her warm and polite reception from black Pullman porters when traveling from Florida to Georgia impressed her equally.[31] Tuggle's references to these common and elite people outside the Church of Christ point to a worldview stretching far beyond her chosen religious community.

Apart from its rich text, however, *Another World Wonder* contains a treasure of one hundred exceptionally rare photographs illuminating both the history of African American Churches of Christ and Tuggle's broader, complex world. Some of the pictures portray family members, while others reveal her close associations with many black members of Churches of Christ. The photos of Alexander Campbell, a leading black preacher in Churches of Christ,[32] Henry Clay and his wife,[33] and Nathaniel Cathey and his wife[34] are impressive and rare images of important figures—former enslaved Africans who emerged as leaders in black Churches of Christ in the late nineteenth and early twentieth centuries. Obscure black preachers such as T. H. Busby,[35] P. H. Black,[36] T. K. Rouse,[37] and J. Tom Daniel,[38] among others, whose names occasionally surfaced in the pages of the *Gospel Advocate* and the *Christian Echo* find a prominent place and a lasting identity in Tuggle's *Another World Wonder.*

Out of the one hundred photographs that compliment Tuggle's work, seven of them picture white people. Even though she intended her book to chronicle her life and the history of African American Churches of Christ, Tuggle clearly perceived the material and spiritual advancement of black Christians as inextricably linked to the assistance of white believers.[39] One picture of a newspaper clipping of former First Lady Eleanor

Roosevelt intimates that Tuggle, like many African Americans in the 1930s, was enamored with the Roosevelts and the Democratic Party, even though the black author never fully disclosed her political affiliation.[40] Notwithstanding her public reticence concerning political matters, Tuggle understood the value of a well-placed photograph.

Another World Wonder demonstrates the seminal role women played in Tuggle's own life as well as in the spiritual formation of black Churches of Christ. From her mother Mollie, who lovingly molded her character, to her oldest sister Gertrude Holmes, who led her into the fold of Churches of Christ, Tuggle had many female friends, mentors, and soul mates. The wife of preacher P. H. Black, Millie Black, an expert domestic, hospitably received her and two other Walden College students into her home.[41] Her Aunt Sophia lent unconditional support after Tuggle's unpopular decision to leave Lane College and enroll at LeMoyne Normal Institute, and her cousin Eunice vowed to help her fulfill her dream of becoming an efficient educator. After relocating to Detroit in 1944, Annie and her sister Irene P. Moody collaborated in a profitable pie-baking business. Her youngest sister, Emma Rushing, helped Tuggle regain her emotional and financial footing after her painful divorce. Throughout her life Annie Tuggle seemed to have a ready coterie of black women from whom to draw needed support, yet at the same time concerned white sisters also stepped forward at critical junctures to provide essential encouragement; among these, the Shappley sisters and Effie White stand as a few among many.[42] And beyond Churches of Christ, Tuggle found friends while holding teaching posts across Tennessee. She especially admired and appreciated Susie Trueheart and Mabel Williams, co-workers at the Prospect School in Germantown, Tennessee.[43]

Beyond the workaday sphere, however, *Another World Wonder* reveals a woman who loved poetry and other literary forms. On three different occasions in her autobiography, Tuggle reflected on the poetry of Edgar Allen Poe. When she ran away from home in 1909, she applied Poe's "The Raven" to her emotional state: "Back into my chamber turning, all my soul within me burning."[44] Certain that her mother, Mollie, would not permit her to transfer to the LeMoyne Normal Institute, Tuggle felt that she was like Poe's black raven in a state of darkness and uncertainty. And when her father, Haywood Tuggle, consented to allow her to enroll at an all-black school in Memphis, in celebration she quoted verses from Rudyard Kipling's poem, "If."[45]

Tuggle dedicated J. T. Franklin's poem, "The Tigers and the Kids," to her Aunt Sophia in recognition of all her untiring support while she studied at LeMoyne Normal Institute.[46] Annie even found herself the subject of a poem when C. A. Nall, Tuggle's former classmate and then principal of the Sanford Vocational and Industrial High School in Seale, Alabama, composed a poem in honor of Tuggle, titling it "The Alabama Tent Meeting."

> Away back yonder some years ago
> Near the other struggle
> I met a lady who was not slow,
> They called her Annie Tuggle

Brother G. P. Bowser had the tent
In which to hold thy meeting
Many of us into it went
While others stood out peeping. . . .

Miss Tuggle rose one night and said
Before they took up the money:
'You people listen; hold up your head;
This meeting is not funny.

Expense belongs to everything
Now people don't get tickled
It's hard to go when you only bring
To this great cause a nickle [sic]

Help keep the meeting going high
Each night it's growing hotter
One nickel you know just will buy
A bottle of soda water

Brother Bowser taught a Bible class,
And made it plain and simple
He said it clear but spoke it fast
With sweat upon his temple.

The miners and the railroad men
Would lean upon their shovels;
Discuss the text while some would grin
And others raise the devil.

The preachers were the first to fight,

The officers, then the rest;
It was not long before every night
He was in a hornet's nest:

Brother Bowser stood his ground just fine,
He would never tuck his head;
But could put his finger on every line,
Of Scripture he had read. . . .

Heneretta Nall was the first to go
Up there and give her hand
Some of them that had been slow
They started to raising sand.

One night in his hand the Bible he took
And to all he did tell
If you don't obey this book! Book! Book!
You will die and go to hell.

In Nashville before leaving Whet Stone Hall
I saw the same Miss Tuggle;
We discussed the details great and small
Of this great Christian struggle[47]

Even though Nall's poem does not reveal the specific time and location of the Alabama gospel meeting, his reference to "miners and railroad men" suggests a Birmingham vicinity, where many black coal miners labored. Nall's verses attest to the seminal role G. P. Bowser played in the Alabama campaign. The references to preachers fighting and "a hornet's nest" imply that his sermons were combative and exclusivistic; consequently, they generated discord and disturbance in this Alabama religious community. Despite the controversy Bowser's passionate, "plain and simple" preaching engendered, it proved effective in that a close relative of the poet, Heneretta Nall, came forward to "give her hand," that is, she became a member of Churches of Christ. It is likely that during this Alabama campaign, C. A. Nall converted to the same fellowship, for he later indicated that he attended the Jefferson Street Church of Christ while a student at Walden College.

More significantly, the verses highlight the contribution that Annie C. Tuggle made to the "Alabama Tent Meeting," as she boldly stood up and challenged those who attended the campaign to generously "help keep the meeting going high." As a loving, caring, yet firm "church mother," Tuggle understood the crucial role that financial support played in spiritual success.

Tuggle also included in her book a poem called "What Must I Do?" which was composed by Addie B. Shappley, a white Christian and close friend of Tuggle. Shappley wrote that:

> If in this world you have silver and gold
> You have friends and fame and pleasures untold;
> But if there's been no place made for Jesus by you
> Ah! My friends it's time you were asking "Lord what
> must I do?"[48]

Taking her cue from Acts 16:30, where the Philippian jailer asked Paul and Silas, "What must I do to be saved?" Addie B. Shappley gave her poem a similar title. The foregoing verses unquestionably appealed to Tuggle because she was never preoccupied with materialistic and monetary gain; her life's goal was to please God.

Irene P. Moody composed one of Tuggle's favorite poems. Entitled the "Pie Lady," the poem celebrated Tuggle's successful culinary business in Detroit.

You look like a May queen
With those million dollar smiles,
But your pies are far better
Than any of your styles. . . .

On the recording machine
You make great speeches,
But the thing that counts
Is your pies made of peaches.

Go on Pie Lady
With your wonderful work,
You have fed the town
On delicious dessert.[49]

In addition to poets, classical authors pervaded Tuggle's mind. Even though she studied Latin and French at Walden College, Greek classical literature impressed her most deeply. While a student at Walden, Tuggle came under the influence of Mattie Carr Chavis, an English instructor who advised her: "Personally, you may never need Algebra, Geometry, Ciscero [*sic*] or Virgil, but the study of them will cause you to think and thought rules the world."[50] Following her mentor's urging Tuggle drew moral lessons from Demosthenes. "History tells us that if the condition under which Demosthenes the Greek Philosopher was born had been as favorable as that provided for [statesman Daniel] Webster, then perhaps Demosthenes was raised almost by himself, with no strong family or religious ties."[51] Tuggle used the story of Demosthenes to urge parents to provide their children with a morally wholesome and physically safe environment. "Parents must do all they can to provide a wholesome Christian environment for their children. The Bible teaches that 'evil companionships corrupt good morals.' (1 Cor. 15:33)."[52] Tuggle quoted Plato to denounce the love of money. "It was Plato who said: 'It was the insatiable craving for wealth and the disregard of everything else for the sake of money-making that destroyed oligarchy.'"[53] But while Tuggle dabbled in classical literature, she found her moral base in God's Word.

Another World Wonder exposes the heart and soul of Annie Tuggle. It discloses her successes as a proud valedictorian at Walden College and as a subsequently influential educator, while simultaneously divulging her disappointments as a divorced and barren woman. She also internalized the failures of G. P. Bowser's Silver Point Christian Institute and Marshall Keeble's Nashville Christian Institute, immersing herself in both of these short-lived endeavors.

Another World Wonder, then, tells the story of Tuggle's life, but much more. It is a most important historical source for understanding the history of African American Churches of Christ. Tuggle both touched and was touched by an exceptionally wide spectrum of white and black leaders in Churches of Christ. She enjoyed the hospitality of preacher, editor, and educator, David Lipscomb. She worked for and with businessman and philanthropist, A. M. Burton. She assisted G. P. Bowser, Marshall Keeble, R. N. Hogan, and other noteworthy black leaders in Churches of Christ. She instructed, encouraged, and mentored aspiring young preachers such as Fred Gray, Kelly K. Mitchell, and Robert Woods, among others.

Tuggle also drew on a broad base in her quest for truth. *Another World Wonder* reveals that to Tuggle all truth was God's truth. Even though she peppered her autobiography with scriptural quotations, she mined secular sources as well for moral lessons. Reflecting on her disappointments, frustrations, and flaws, Tuggle looked to Abraham Lincoln as a source of inspiration. "Few men in public or private life met with the series of disappointments as did Abraham Lincoln, and yet he was not discouraged. Defeat to him was simply and invitation to greater efforts." Although the sixteenth president of the United States was "cut down as a flower at the height of his fame," Tuggled noted that "he left on record a life lesson—Keep Trying."[54] A principal theme of her autobiography was clearly perseverance. The primary message, nevertheless, was that she consistently recognized God's leading and direction of every aspect of her life. After J. H. Lovell, president of Walden College, surprisingly appointed her dining hall and dormitory supervisor "with pay," Tuggle prayed: "Dear heavenly Father, to the extent of my brain power, I realize your presence and all it is in me to comprehend of your power. Help me to learn even this late lessons of your wonderful creations. Help me to unshackle and expand my soul to the fullest realization of your wonders. Amen." Notwithstanding her failures and frustrations, Tuggle lived a life full of "wonders" for she possessed the uncanny ability to see and sense the power and presence of God in all her dealings and in all his "wonderful creations."

EPILOGUE

THE LEGACY OF ANNIE C. TUGGLE

Annie C. Tuggle died in 1976, as the United States was celebrating its bicentennial birth of freedom. The year was significant for the nation for other reasons as well. Political transitions, technological and transportation developments, and social advances stamped a memorable year. The nation inaugurated it thirty-ninth chief executive, Jimmy Carter, the first president from the Deep South since the Civil War. In 1976 Mao Tse-tung, the Communist leader of China, died after more than a two-decade rule. Apple launched its first computer; VCRs were released; CB radios became a national craze; and the first Concord supersonic airliner made its transatlantic commercial flight. Opening prominent positions to females in the armed services, West Point military academy admitted 119 women in this exceptional American year.

Annie C. Tuggle passed away, however, with no fanfare, parade, or lying in state to commemorate her impressive life. Reared in a loving and devout family in West Tennessee, Tuggle moved about with confidence, assured that she was doing God's will and committed to improving her own life and the life of American blacks. Like many other African Americans, she understood that education was the key to social and material advancement. When observing how diligently she studied in preparing to pass the Tennessee state teachers exam, professor Whiteside remarked, "Miss Tuggle, you have the tenacity of a bulldog and I believe you are going to make a first-grade certificate."[1] Tuggle's tenacious disposition inspired her to persevere at three different colleges until she earned her bachelor's degree at the age of thirty-three. Upon graduating as valedictorian from Walden College, she immediately set out to lift up African American youth, particularly those in Churches of Christ. Tuggle's faith in God empowered her and enabled her to withstand a failed marriage, health problems, and financial woes, which tempered her optimism but did not dash it.

Tuggle's commitment first and foremost was to the growth, expansion, and strengthening of African American Churches of Christ, whom she believed possessed "the truth" and into which she poured her heart and soul as an educator, historian, and indefatigable supporter. She read scripture for preachers who needed assistance; she answered biblical questions when ministers were stumped; she counseled white and black leaders when they found themselves in dilemmas; she warded off illicit sexual advances from white predators; and she helped preserve the history of African American Churches of Christ in her collection of biographical sketches, *Our Ministers and Songleaders of the Church of Christ,* and her unadulterated autobiography, *Another World*

Wonder. Most importantly Tuggle realized that without a past there was no historical base for herself and or her people.

Those who best knew Tuggle clearly understood her significance. In a personal letter Ella Steward, a close friend of Tuggle, observed that Annie's "power and influence" were known across "the brotherhood" of African American Churches of Christ, not because she left behind lavish buildings of "mortar and stone" bearing her name, but because of her sacrifices and because of the countless numbers of lives she had touched and transformed.[2] In Steward's estimation, Tuggle possessed a natural talent for garnering financial support for the cause of Christ and helped the Iowa and Lauderdale Church of Christ in Memphis to pay off "the last note on the mother congregation there." Steward never forgot Tuggle's sacrificial commitment, and she understood that Tuggle's "power and influence" extended far beyond West Tennessee and pervaded the "brotherhood" of African American Churches of Christ in the United States, even carrying over into the West Indies.

Steward was not alone in her commendation of Tuggle. Marshall Keeble, the most preeminent evangelist in Churches of Christ, lauded Tuggle as a true servant of God. In the early 1940s, when philanthropist A. M. Burton searched extensively for a dedicated Christian educator for the Nashville Christian Institute, Keeble "suggested to him to send and get Annie Tuggle for one of the teachers, to be sure he would have a Christian teacher in a Christian institution."[3] Tuggle's biblical knowledge, spiritual commitment, moral purity, and selfless spirit deeply impressed the great evangelist. Even though her dreams of having children vanished after her divorce, Tuggle gave birth to multiple spiritual progeny such as civil rights attorney Fred D. Gray, preacher Robert Woods, and evangelist Woodie Morrison among many others who have left a lasting imprint on African American Churches of Christ and beyond. Even though Tuggle departed this world without a flamboyant funeral and largely unknown, her tenacious spirit lives on in the young people whom she taught and mentored in the NCI and in her autobiography, *Another World Wonder*.

Annie C. Tuggle once applauded and appraised Marshall Keeble, observing that he was "as brave as a lion and as humble as a lamb."[4] With this statement, Tuggle assessed Keeble's dual and compelling personality, gentle and kind among those who needed his compassionate touch, but fierce and unrelenting when circumstances demanded his remarkable strength. Tuggle's evaluation of Keeble fitted her own persona equally well. She was a complex woman who survived and thrived in a complicated and tumultuous world, a world she would not allow to crush her as she clung unshakably to her faith and integrity with "the tenacity of a bulldog."

APPENDIX

A CHRONOLOGY OF ANNIE C. TUGGLE

1890	Annie C. Tuggle near Germantown, TN
1894	Grandfather's (Haywood Tuggle) house burned
1908	Converted from Methodism to Churches of Christ; Baptized by Robert Burton
1908	Led worship for Smyrna Church of Christ—an all female congregation in Germantown, TN
1908	Attended Lane College in Jackson, TN
1909	Ran away from home
1910	Enrolled in LeMoyne Normal Institute in Memphis, TN
1911	Began teaching at the Prospect School in Memphis, TN
1913	Traveled to Nashville, TN, and met Marshall Keeble; Began studying under G. P. Bowser at the Silver Point Christian Institute (SPCI) in Silver Point, TN
1914	Traveled across TN, MS, and AR to raise funds for the SPCI
1916	Left SPCI
1916	Appointed Principal at Richmond School near Shelbyville, TN
1920	Asked by A. M. Burton to canvass for the Southern Practical Institute in Nashville, TN; the school closed abruptly
1920	Enrolled at Walden College in Nashville, TN
1923	Graduated Valedictorian from Walden College
1923-1924	Attended Fisk University in Nashville, TN
1924-1925	Attended Tennessee A & I State College in Nashville, TN
1925	Walden College closed
1925	Appointed Principal at Hamner Taylor School near Memphis, TN
1927	Married Dr. John Waller

1932	Divorced Dr. John Waller
1932	Influenced white and black leaders of Churches of Christ in Memphis, TN, to invite Marshall Keeble for a preaching campaign
1932-1942	Resided in Memphis, TN, and served as a Bible class teacher for women at the Iowa and Lauderdale Church of Christ
1943-1944	Worked as a teacher at the Nashville Christian Institute in Nashville, TN
1944-1964	Resided in Detroit, MI, where she worked in insurance sales-lady and pie-lady
1945	Published *Our Ministers and Song Leaders of the Church of Christ*
1946	Established the Home Training Christian Institute in Detroit, MI
1947	Fannie R. Bowser, wife of G. P. Bowser, Died
1950	G. P. Bowser, founding editor of the *Christian Echo*, died
1964-1971	Resided in Memphis, TN
1967	Traveled to the Bahamas, Jamaica, and Haiti to do missionary work
1968	Martin Luther King Jr. died in Memphis, TN, and Marshall Keeble died in Nashville, TN
1971	Relocated to Perris, CA
1973	Published *Another World Wonder*
1976	Died in Perris, CA

NOTES

Prologue

1. W. E. B. Du Bois, "The Damnation of Women" [1920], in *W. E. B. Du Bois: A Reader*, ed. David Levering Lewis (New York: Henry Holt, 1995), 308.

2. The Restoration Movement or the Stone-Campbell Movement, which sought to "restore" New Testament Christianity in the modern era, emerged on North American soil in the early nineteenth century largely through the diligent and zealous efforts of four principal leaders: Barton W. Stone (1772–1844), Thomas Campbell (1763–1854), Alexander Campbell (1788–1866), and Walter Scott (1796–1861). For insightful studies of the Stone-Campbell Movement, see James DeForest Murch, *Christians Only: A History of the Restoration Movement* (Cincinnati, OH.: Standard Publishing, 1962); Leroy Garrett, *The Stone-Campbell Movement: An Anecdotal History of Three Churches* (Joplin, MO.: College Press, 1987 [1981]); Richard T. Hughes, *Reviving the Ancient Faith: The Story of Churches of Christ in America* (Grand Rapids, MI.: Eerdmans, 1996); Douglas A. Foster, Paul M. Blowers, Anthony L. Dunnavant, and D. Newell Williams, eds., *The Encyclopedia of the Stone-Campbell Movement* (Grand Rapids, MI.: Eerdmans, 2004).

3. J. E. Choate, *Roll Jordan Roll: A Biography of Marshall Keeble* (Nashville, TN.: Gospel Advocate Company, 1974); R. Vernon Boyd, *Undying Dedication: The Story of G. P. Bowser* (Nashville, TN.: Gospel Advocate Company, 1985); Calvin H. Bowers, *Realizing the California Dream: The Story of the Black Churches of Christ in Los Angeles* (Calvin H. Bowers, 2001); Edward J. Robinson, *Show Us How You Do It: Marshall Keeble and the Rise of Black Churches of Christ in the United States, 1914–1968* (Tuscaloosa: University of Alabama Press, 2008); Edward J. Robinson, *The Fight Is on in Texas: A History of African American Churches of Christ in the Lone Star State, 1865–2000* (Abilene, TX.: Abilene Christian University Press, 2008).

There have been, however, a few historians who have noted Annie C. Tuggle's importance in African American Churches of Christ. See Michael W. Casey, "Annie C. Tuggle: Historian and Educator for the Black Churches of Christ," *Leaven* 3 (1995): 47–48; and Richard T. Hughes and R. L. Roberts, *The Churches of Christ* (Westport, CT.: Greenwood, 2001), 311–12.

4. Annie C. Tuggle, *Another World Wonder* (n.p., n.d.), 45.

5. Deborah Gray White, *Ar'n't I a Woman?: Female Slaves in the Plantation South* (New York: W. W. Norton, 1985), 23.

6. Jacqueline Jones, *Labor of Love, Labor of Sorrow: Black Women, Work, and the Family, from Slavery to the Present* (New York: Vintage Books, 1986), 3.

7. Cynthia Neverdon-Morton, *Afro-American Women of the South and the Advancement of the Race, 1895–1925* (Knoxville: University of Tennessee Press, 1989), 9.

8. Cynthia Griggs Fleming, *Soon We Will Not Cry: The Liberation of Ruby Doris Smith Robinson* (Lanham, MD.: Rowman & Littlefield, 1998), 118.

9. Alice Walker defines a womanist as one who "appreciates and prefers women's culture, women's emotional flexibility . . . and women's strength. Sometimes loves individual men, sexually and/or nonsexually. Committed to survival and wholeness of entire people, male *and* female. Not a separatist, except periodically, for health." See Walker, *In Search of Our Mothers' Gardens* (San Diego: Harcourt Brace Jovanovich, 1983 [1967]), xi. While all of Walker's definitions of womanist might not apply to Annie C. Tuggle, the statement about commitment "to survival and wholeness of entire people" certainly does.

10. Hughes, *Reviving the Ancient Faith,* xiii, defines a sect as a "religious organization that insists that it—and it alone—constitutes the entirety of the kingdom of God." See also Ernst Troeltsch, *The Social Teaching of the Christian Churches* (New York: MacMillan, 1950 [1931]), 1:333–43.

11. Fanning Tolbert and David Lipscomb established the *Gospel Advocate* in 1855. With the exception of a four-year hiatus (1861–1865) during the American Civil War, the journal has been continuously published up until the present. See Earl West, *The Life and Times of David Lipscomb* (Germantown, TN.: Religious Book Service, 1987); Robert Hooper, *Crying in the Wilderness: A Biography of David Lipscomb* (Nashville, TN.: David Lipscomb College, 1979); David L. Little, "Gospel Advocate," in *Encyclopedia of the Stone-Campbell Movement*, 361–63.

12. Samuel Robert Cassius, "My Trip to the East," *Christian Leader* 36 (June 20, 1922): 12. Edward J. Robinson, *To Save My Race from Abuse: The Life of Samuel Robert Cassius* (Tuscaloosa: University of Alabama Press, 2007), 164.

13. Willie Cato, "Keeble as a Teacher," *Gospel Advocate* 110 (May 2, 1968): 452.

14. Recently, historian Curtis J. Evans, *The Burden of Black Religion* (New York: Oxford University Press, 2008), 5, has insightfully observed that "'Black religion,' whether conceptualized variously by whites and blacks as an amorphous spirituality, primitive religion, emotionalism, or actual black churches under the rubric of 'the Negro Church,' groaned under the burden of a multiplicity of interpreters' demands ranging from uplift of the race to bringing an ambiguous quality of 'spiritual softness' to a materialistic and racist white culture." Even though Evans's insightful and nuanced study does not encompass African Americans in Churches of Christ, many of his observations about whites' racial and racist assumptions of black people as well as black Christians' rejection of the "excessive emotionalism" (171) exhibited by many black religionists certainly apply to Annie C. Tuggle and other blacks in Churches of Christ. For Tuggle's preference for a religion with "no whooping and hollering," see Tuggle, *Another World Wonder,* 12. See also B. C. Goodpasture, *Marshall Keeble: Biography and Sermons* (Nashville, TN.: Gospel Advocate Company, 1966 [1931]), 38; and Robinson, *To Save My Race from Abuse,* 145.

Additionally, Virginia Foster Durr (1903–1999), a daughter of white prominent leaders from Birmingham, Alabama, and a contemporary of Annie C. Tuggle, captured the struggles African Americans shouldered in the post–Civil War era, noting that the "white people were telling the black people that in their own person they were unattractive, that they were ugly and black and smelled bad and were probably diseased. That's a terrible burden for people to bear." See Hollinger F. Barnard, ed., *Outside the Magic Circle: The Autobiography of Virginia Foster Durr* (Tuscaloosa: University of Alabama Press, 1986), 253.

15. Annie C. Tuggle, "Among the Colored People," *Gospel Advocate* 63 (February 3, 1921): 125.

16. Even though the words of Evelyn Brooks Higginbotham, *Righteous Discontent: The Women's Movement in the Black Baptist Church, 1880–1920* (Cambridge, MA.: Harvard University Press, 1981), 1, apply primarily to African American women in Baptist Churches during the Gilded Age and Progressive era, her observation fits Tuggle extremely well.

17. Deborah Gray White, *Too Heavy a Load: Black Women in Defense of Themselves, 1894–1994* (New York: W. W. Norton, 1999), 16.

18. Cheryl Gilkes, *If It Wasn't for the Women: Black Women's Experience and Womanist Culture in Church and Community* (Maryknoll, N.Y.: Orbis Books, 2001).

Chapter 1

1. Sarah Dudley Pettey, "What Role is the Educated Negro Woman to Play in the Uplifting of Her Race?" [1870s], in *Can I Get A Witness?: Prophetic Religious Voices of African American Women: An Anthology*, ed. Marcia Y. Riggs (Maryknoll, N.Y.: Orbis Books, 1997), 79.

2. For the Tom Moss quote, see Alfreda M. Duster, ed., *Crusade for Justice: The Autobiography of Ida B. Wells* (Chicago: University of Chicago Press, 1970), 50–51; Linda O. McMurry, *To Keep the Waters Troubled: The Life of Ida B. Wells* (New York: Oxford University Press, 1998), 133, 143. For the number of lynchings in the early 1890s, see Philip Dray, *At the Hands of Persons Unknown: The Lynching of Black America* (New York: Modern Library, 2003), viii; Paula J. Giddings, *Ida, A Sword among Lions: Ida B. Wells and the Campaign against Lynching* (New York: Amistad, 2008), 185. For an assessment of the plight of African Americans in Tennessee, see Lester C. Lamon, *Black Tennesseans, 1900–1930* (Knoxville: University of Tennessee Press, 1977), 231. For a discussion of race relations in post–Civil War Memphis, see Beverly Greene Bond, "'Till Fair Aurora Rise': African American Women in Memphis, Tennessee, 1840–1915" (PhD dissertation, University of Memphis, 1996), 69–103.

3. John Hope Franklin and Alfred A. Moss Jr., *From Slavery to Freedom: A History of African Americans* (Boston: McGraw, 2000 [1947]), 290; C. Vann Woodward, *Origins of the New South* (Baton Rouge: Louisiana State University Press, 1997 1951]), 211, 212, 353–55.

4. Mark W. Summers, *The Gilded Age, or the Hazard of New Functions* (Upper Saddle River, N.J.: Prentice, 1997), 236, 240.

5. Anna Rochester, *The Populist Movement in the United States* (New York: International Publishers, 1943), 35; Summers, *The Gilded Age*, 223–25.

6. Summers, *The Gilded Age*, 268–70.

7. Rudyard Kipling, "The White Man's Burden," in *Rudyard Kipling's Verse* (New York: Doubleday, Doran, 1945), 321–23. See also, Nell Irvin Painter, *Standing at Armageddon: The United States, 1877–1919* (New York: W. W. Norton, 1987), 141–69.

8. Annie C. Tuggle, *Another World Wonder* (n.p., n.d.), 1; Barbara Jeanne Fields, *Slavery and Freedom on the Middle Ground: Maryland during the Nineteenth Century* (New Haven, CT.: Yale University Press, 1985), 2.

9. Frederick Douglass, *My Bondage and My Freedom* (New York: Dover, 1969 [1855]), 61, noted: "It is generally supposed that slavery, in the state of Maryland, exists in its mildest form, and that it is totally divested of those harsh and terrible peculiarities, which mark and characterize the slave system, in the southern and south-western states of the American union."

10. Frederick Douglass, *Narrative of the Life of Frederick Douglass, An American Slave* (New York: Penguin Books, 1986 [1845]), 90. For an example of an enslaved woman from Maryland, Eliza, who was separated from her daughter, Jennie, and was sold to Louisiana, yet pled with her former owner to restore to her daughter, see Kenneth M. Stampp, *The Peculiar Institution: Slavery in the Antebellum South* (New York: Vintage Books, 1956), 242–43.

11. Tuggle, *Another World Wonder*, 1. For Methodism's appeal to prosperous white slaveholders, see James Oakes, *The Ruling Race: A History of American Slaveholders* (New York: Knopf, 1982), 97.

12. In 1850, Maryland claimed 90,368 slaves; Tennessee claimed 239,459. A decade later, Maryland reported having 87,189 slaves, while Tennessee boasted owning 275,719 slaves. See Fields, 2; and Peter Kolchin, *American Slavery, 1619–1877* (New York: Hill and Wang, 1993), 242.

13. 1860 United States Federal Census (Shelby County, Tennessee).

14. Local newspapers of Shelby County, Tennessee, portray Phillip Tuggle Sr. as an influential Methodist minister, busily traversing West Tennessee, preaching sermons, performing weddings, and conducting funerals. See *Daily Memphis Enquirer* (September 5, 1848); *Memphis Daily Appeal* (October 27, 1855); *Memphis Daily Appeal* (December 23, 1855); *Memphis Daily Appeal* (March 17, 1857); *Memphis Daily Appeal* (August 5, 1857); *Memphis Daily Appeal* (December 25, 1857). See also Helen Rowland, *Shelby County, Tennessee Newspaper Abstracts through 1859* (Signal Mountain, TN.: Mountain Press, 2002), 39, 181, 182, 236, 267, 271.

15. 1860 United States Federal Census: Slave Schedules (Shelby County, Tennessee). For a useful background study of the slave population of Memphis, Tennessee, see Kathleen Christine Berkeley, "'Like A Plague of Locust': Immigration and Social Change in Memphis, Tennessee, 1850–1880" (PhD dissertation, University of California, Los Angeles, 1980), 7–60.

16. Tuggle, *Another World Wonder*, 1.

17. Albert J. Raboteau, *Slave Religion: The "Invisible Institution" in the Antebellum South* (New York: Oxford University Press, 1978), 130–33; Lewis V. Baldwin, *"Invisible" Strands in African Methodism: A History of the African Union Methodist and American Methodist Episcopal Churches, 1805–1980* (Metuchen, N.J.: Scarecrow Press, 1983), 18–19; Nathan O. Hatch, *The Democratization of American Christianity* (New Haven, CT.: Yale University Press, 1989), 102–5. See also Richard S. Newman, *Freedom's Prophet: Bishop Richard Allen, the AME Church and the Black Founding Fathers* (New York: New York University Press, 2008).

18. Tuggle, *Another World Wonder*, 2. The emergence of black property-owners in the late nineteenth and early twentieth centuries has been well documented by scholar Loren Schweninger, *Black Property Owners in the South, 1790–1915* (Urbana: University of Illinois Press, 1990), 184.

19. 1850 United States Federal Census: Slave Schedules (Shelby County, Tennessee); Tuggle, *Another World Wonder*, 2.

20. Tuggle, *Another World Wonder*, 2.

21. Solomon Northup, *Twelve Years a Slave* (Mineola, N.Y.: Dover, 1970 [1853]), 199.

22. Joshua D. Rothman, *Notorious in the Neighborhood: Sex and Family across the Color Line in Virginia, 1787–1861* (Chapel Hill: University of North Carolina Press, 2003).

23. Herbert G. Gutman, *The Black Family in Slavery and Freedom, 1750–1925* (New York: Vintage Books, 1976), 388–96; John W. Blassingame, *The Slave Community: Plantation Life in the Antebellum South* (New York: Oxford University Press, 1979 [1972]), 155–56.

24. Tuggle, *Another World Wonder*, 2.

25. Howard Bodenhorn, "The Mulatto Advantage: The Biological Consequences in Rural Antebellum Virginia," *Journal of Interdisciplinary History* 33 (Summer 2002): 21–46.

26. Tuggle, *Another World Wonder*, 3.

27. Ishmell Hendrex Edwards, "A History of Rust College" (PhD dissertation, University of Mississippi, 1993), 1.

28. Tuggle, *Another World Wonder*, 3.

29. Tuggle, *Another World Wonder*, 6–7.

30. Teresa L. Fry Brown, *God Don't Like Ugly: African American Women Handing on Spiritual Values* (Nashville, TN.: Abingdon, 2000).

31. Tuggle, *Another World Wonder*, 7.

32. Tuggle, *Another World Wonder*, 6.

33. Tuggle, *Another World Wonder*, 59.

34. Tuggle, *Another World Wonder*, 8.

35. Tuggle, *Another World Wonder*, 8.

Chapter 2

1. Lucy Craft Laney, "The Burden of the Educated Colored Woman," *Report of the Hampton Negro Conference* (July 1899), 37, 42.

2. Ibid. See also Britt Edward Cottingham, "The Burden of the Educated Colored Woman: Lucy Laney and Haines Institute, 1886–1933" (Masters thesis, Georgia State University, 1995).

3. Annie C. Tuggle, *Another World Wonder* (n.p., n.d.). The quote is from Tuggle's Introduction and there are no page numbers.

4. Tuggle, *Another World Wonder*, 10.

5. Walter Scott, a co-laborer of Alexander Campbell in the early nineteenth century, devised the "plan of salvation" with a six-finger exercise, equally emphasizing man's response—believing, repenting, and being immersed—to God's work of forgiving sins, bestowing the gift of the Holy Spirit, and granting the gift of eternal life. By the late nineteenth century, Scott's six-finger exercise had been modified and legalized to a five-step plan which stressed primarily man's work—hearing the Gospel, believing

the Gospel, repenting of one's sins, confessing the name of Christ, and being baptized for the remission of sins. Annie C. Tuggle came over into Churches of Christ after the latter plan, which by the early twentieth century had become prevalent in Tennessee and other southern states where Churches of Christ were numerically strong. See Richard T. Hughes, *Reviving the Ancient Faith: The Story of Churches of Christ in America* (Grand Rapids, MI.: Eerdmans, 1996): 50-52.

6. Tuggle, *Another World Wonder*, 10–11.

7. Horace C. Savage, *Life and Times of Bishop Isaac Lane* (Nashville, TN.: National Publication Company, 1958), 124; C. H. Phillips, *The History of the Colored Methodist Episcopal Church in America* (New York: Arno, 1972), 121; Paul R. Griffin, "Black Founders of Reconstruction Era Methodist Colleges: Daniel A. Payne, Joseph C. Price, and Isaac Lane, 1863–1890" (PhD dissertation, Emory University, 1983), 73, 85–86.

8. Tuggle, *Another World Wonder*, 21.

9. Alicia K. Jackson, "The Colored Methodist Episcopal Church and Their Struggle for Autonomy and Reform in the New South" (PhD dissertation, University of Mississippi, 2004), 60.

10. Tuggle, *Another World Wonder*, 21.

11. Tuggle, *Another World Wonder*, 22.

12. Tuggle, *Another World Wonder*, 22. For an insightful discussion of the "color complex," see Kathy Russell, Midge Wilson, and Ronald Hall, *The Color Complex: The Politics of Skin Color among African Americans* (New York: Harcourt Brace Jovanovich, 1992). The authors of *The Color Complex* define the "color complex" as a "psychological fixation about color and features that leads Blacks to discriminate against each other." The conflict between lighter-skinned and darker-skinned blacks in the Progressive era has been thoroughly documented by Willard B. Gatewood, *Aristocrats of Color: The Black Elite, 1880–1920* (Bloomington: Indiana University Press, 1990), 152.

13. Tuggle, *Another World Wonder*, 23.

14. Tuggle, *Another World Wonder*, 25.

15. Tuggle, *Another World Wonder*, 13. Annie C. Tuggle, like many of her black contemporaries in Churches of Christ, was a "radical exclusivist," who insisted that God rejected Baptists, Methodists, Pentecostals, and other religious groups who received baptism without understanding that it was "for the remission of sins." When these unsaved people learn the true purpose of baptism, they must be rebaptized; this baptism makes them true Christians and places them into the one true church—the Churches of Christ. See C. Myer Phillips, "A Historical Study of the Attitude of the Churches of Christ toward Other Denominations" (PhD dissertation, Baylor University, 1983), 47–83.

16. Tuggle, *Another World Wonder*, 25.

17. Ruth Rosen, *The Lost Sisterhood: Prostitution in America, 1900–1918* (Baltimore, MD.: Johns Hopkins University Press, 1982), 15. See also, Lois W. Banner, *Women in Modern America: A Brief History* (San Diego: Harcourt Brace Jovanovich, 1984 [1974]), 82, 85.

18. Katie N. Johnson, *Sisters in Sin: Brothel Drama in America, 1900–1920* (New York: Cambridge University Press, 2006), 1.

19. Mark Thomas Connelly, *The Response to Prostitution in the Progressive Era* (Chapel Hill: University of North Carolina Press, 1980), 115.

20. Mary E. Odem, *Delinquent Daughters: Protecting and Policing Adolescent Female Sexuality in the United States, 1885–1920* (Chapel Hill: University of North Carolina Press, 1996).

21. Robert A. Sigafoos, *Cotton Row to Beale Street: A Business History of Memphis* (Memphis: Memphis State University Press, 1979), 173.

22. Fred L. Hutchins, *What Happened in Memphis* (Kingsport, TN.: Kingsport Press, 1965), 43, 44.

23. Tuggle, *Another World Wonder*, 25.

24. Tuggle, *Another World Wonder*, 27–28.

25. Tuggle, *Another World Wonder*, 29.

26. Tuggle, *Another World Wonder*, 29, 35.

27. Tuggle, *Another World Wonder*, 37.

28. Tuggle, *Another World Wonder*, 37.

29. Tuggle, *Another World Wonder*, 40.

30. Tuggle, *Another World Wonder*, 40.

31. Tuggle, *Another World Wonder*, 41.

32. Tuggle, *Another World Wonder*, 44.

33. R. Vernon Boyd, *Undying Dedication: The Story of G. P. Bowser* (Nashville, TN.: Gospel Advocate Company, 1985), 45.

34. Tuggle, *Another World Wonder*, 46.

35. Paula Giddings, *Ida, A Sword among Lions: Ida B. Wells and the Campaign against Lynching* (New York: Amistad, 2008), 4; Linda O. McMurry, *To Keep the Waters Troubled: The Life of Ida B. Wells* (New York: Oxford University Press, 1998), 13–14.

36. Chana Kai Lee, *For Freedom's Sake: The Life of Fannie Lou Hamer* (Urbana: University of Illinois Press, 1999), 16.

37. Samuel Robert Cassius, "An Appreciation of Booker T. Washington," *Gospel Advocate* 58 (December 23, 1915): 1302; and Edward J. Robinson, *To Save My Race from Abuse: The Life of Samuel Robert Cassius* (Tuscaloosa: University of Alabama Press, 2007), 98. For the Tuggle quote, see Annie C. Tuggle, "Another Appreciation of Booker T. Washington," *Gospel Advocate* 58 (March 30, 1916): 325.

38. Annie C. Tuggle, "A Vision of Opportunity," *Gospel Advocate* 63 (September 1, 1921): 828; see also Tuggle, "Another Appreciation of Booker T. Washington," 325.

39. Annie C. Tuggle, "Among the Colored People," *Gospel Advocate* 58 (July 13, 1916): 718.

40. James R. Grossman, *Land of Hope: Chicago, Black Southerners, and the Great Migration* (Chicago: University of Chicago Press, 1989).

41. Tuggle, *Another World Wonder*, 61; James Weldon Johnson, *The Autobiography of an Ex-Colored Man* (New York: Penguin Books, 1990 [1912]), 40. See also Lawrence W.

Levine, *Black Culture and Black Consciousness: Afro-American Folk Thought from Slavery to Freedom* (New York: Oxford University Press, 1978), 299.

42. Tuggle, *Another World Wonder,* 62–63.

43. Tuggle, *Another World Wonder,* 65–66.

44. Tuggle, *Another World Wonder,* 66. For the front door prohibition that pervaded the South, see Anne Moody, *Coming of Age in Mississippi* (New York: Laurel Book, 1968), 117; Benjamin E. Mays, *Born to Rebel: An Autobiography* (New York: Charles Scribner's Sons, 1971), 46–47.

45. Boyd, *Undying Dedication,* 66; Calvin H. Bowers, *Realizing the California Dream: The Story of the Black Churches of Christ in Los Angeles* (Calvin H. Bowers, 2001), 75–76.

46. Edward J. Robinson, *The Fight Is on in Texas: A History of African American Churches of Christ in the Lone Star State, 1865–2000* (Abilene, TX.: Abilene Christian University Press, 2008), 119–34; Robert E. Hooper, *A Distinct People: A History of the Churches of Christ in the 20th Century* (West Monroe, LA.: Howard Publishing, 1993), 260–61.

47. Tuggle, *Another World Wonder,* 66.

48. Annie C. Tuggle, "Among the Colored Folks," *Gospel Advocate* 63 (February 3, 1921): 125.

49. Tuggle, *Another World Wonder,* 66.

50. When Walden University closed its doors in 1925, it lay vacant for a decade before being taken over by Trevecca University. See Mildred Bangs Wynkoop, *The Trevecca Story: 75 Years of Christian Service* (Nashville, TN.: Trevecca Press, 1976), 162–63. Tuggle, *Another World Wonder,* 68–69, 75.

Chapter 3

1. A Southern Colored Woman, "The Race Problem—An Autobiography," *The Independent* 56 (March 17, 1904) in *Black Women in White America: A Documentary History,* ed. Gerda Lerner (New York: Vintage Books, 1972), 158.

2. Harriet A. Jacobs, *Incidents in the Life of a Slave Girl, Written by Himself* (Cambridge, MA.: Harvard University Press, 1987 [1861]), 56; Dorothy Sterling, ed., *We Are Your Sisters: Black Women in the Nineteenth Century* (New York: W. W. Norton, 1997 [1984]), 23.

3. Jacobs, *Incidents in the Life of a Slave Girl,* 77.

4. A Southern Colored Woman, "The Race Problem," 158–59.

5. A Negro nurse, "More Slavery at the South," *The Independent* 72 (January 25, 1912); cited in Gerda Lerner, ed., *Black Women in White America,* 155–57.

6. Douglas A. Blackmon, *Slavery by Another Name: The Re-Enslavement of Black Americans from the Civil War to World War II* (New York: Anchor Books, 2009), 169. The black child whom Strom Thurmond fathered with Carrie Butler, a sixteen-year-old house servant, was Essie Mae Washington-Williams. See Jack Bass and W. Scott Poole, *The Palmetto State: The Making of Modern South Carolina* (Columbia: University of South Carolina Press, 2009), xi, 41, 136, 205.

7. Endesha Ida Mae Holland, *From the Mississippi Delta: A Memoir* (Chicago: Lawrence Hill Brooks, 1997), 85.

8. Annie C. Tuggle, *Another World Wonder* (n.p., n.d.), 17.

9. Grace Elizabeth Hale, *Making Whiteness: The Culture of Segregation in the South, 1890–1940* (New York: Pantheon Books, 1998).

10. Mary Frances Berry and John W. Blassingame, *Long Memory: The Black Experience in America* (New York: Oxford University Press, 1982), 115. See also Paula J. Giddings, *When and Where I Enter: The Impact of Black Women on Race and Sex in America* (New York: William Morrow, 1984), 86; Deborah Gray White, *Ar'n't I a Woman?: Female Slaves in the Plantation South* (New York: W. W. Norton, 1985),164.

11. Cole Blease cited in Douglas A. Blackmon, *Slavery by Another Name*, 305.

12. C. Kendrick, "The Freed People of the South," *Christian Standard* 3 (August 29, 1868): 274; J. W. Crenshaw, "Difficulties in Christianizing the Colored Race," *Christian Standard* 15 (February 28, 1880): 66. See also, David Edwin Harrell, *Sources of Division in the Disciples of Christ, 1865–1900: A Social History of the Disciples of Christ* (Tuscaloosa: University of Alabama Press, 2003 [1973]), 207.

13. John M. McCaleb, "Japan Letter—A Plea for the Colored Man," *Christian Leader and the Way* 21 (January 1, 1907): 2.

14. John M. McCaleb, "Japan Letter—How to Reach the Colored Man," *Christian Leader and the Way* 21 (September 3, 1907): 3.

15. *Thirty Years of Lynching in the United States, 1889–1918* (New York: Arno, 1969), 7.

16. Dray, *At the Hands of Persons Unknown*, 103–4, 245–46.

17. For a white member in the Stone-Campbell Movement who expressed delight over the brutal execution of Sam Hose in Georgia in 1899, see Edward J. Robinson, *To Save My Race from Abuse: The Life of Samuel Robert Cassius* (Tuscaloosa: University of Alabama Press, 2007), 67.

18. Tuggle, *Another World Wonder*, 17.

19. Tuggle, *Another World Wonder*, 96.

20. Andre Tuttle Kornbluh, "'The Bowl of Promise': Cincinnati Social Welfare Planners, Cultural Pluralism and the Metropolitan Community, 1911–1952" (PhD dissertation, University of Cincinnati, 1988), 59.

21. William Wayne Griffin, "The Negro in Ohio" (PhD dissertation, Ohio State University, 1968), 144.

22. Kornbluh, "The Bowl of Promise," 357.

23. Beverly A. Bunch-Lyons, "And They Came: The Migration of African-American Women from the South to Cincinnati, Ohio, 1900–1950" (PhD dissertation, Miami University, 1995), 130.

24. Bunch-Lyons, "And They Came," 116.

25. Tuggle, *Another World Wonder*, 96.

26. Tuggle, *Another World Wonder*, 97.

27. Amity Shlaes, *The Forgotten Man: A New History of the Great Depression* (New York: HarperCollins, 2007), 113.

28. Tuggle, *Another World Wonder*, 97.

29. Tuggle, *Another World Wonder*, 97–98.

30. Tuggle, *Another World Wonder*, 98–99.

31. Tuggle, *Another World Wonder*, 101.

32. For the popularity of Lysol as a contraceptive during the Great Depression, see Ellen Chesler, *Woman of Valor: Margaret Sanger and the Birth Control Movement in America* (New York: Simon & Schuster, 1992), 271. See page 298 for the story of Clarence Gamble, a graduate of Harvard Medical School and professor at the University of Pennsylvania Medical School, who in 1929 helped launch a birth control clinic in his hometown of Cincinnati, Ohio. Matthew Connelly, *Fatal Misconception: The Struggle to Control World Population* (Cambridge, MA.: Harvard University Press, 2008), 83, points out that the birth control industry in the United States soared during the Great Depression and by 1938, the industry had a $250 million market.

33. Tuggle, *Another World Wonder*, 101.

34. Tuggle, *Another World Wonder*, 101, 102.

35. Tuggle, *Another World Wonder*, 126.

36. Tuggle, *Another World Wonder*, 127.

37. Tuggle, *Another World Wonder*, 127–29.

38. Giddings, *When and Where I Enter*, 86.

39. Tuggle, *Another World Wonder*, 129.

Chapter 4

1. Annie C. Tuggle, *Another World Wonder* (n.p., n.d.), 101.

2. Tuggle, *Another World Wonder*, 102.

3. Tuggle, *Another World Wonder*, 89–90.

4. Tuggle, *Another World Wonder*, 102.

5. Tuggle, *Another World Wonder*, 102.

6. Tuggle, *Another World Wonder*, 103.

7. Ray Stannard Baker, *Following the Color Line: American Negro Citizenship in the Progressive Era* (New York: Harper & Row, 1964 [1908]), 81. See also Neil R. McMillan, *Dark Journey: Black Mississippians in the Age of Jim Crow* (Urbana: University of Illinois Press, 1990), 272, who observes that the exodus of black southerners from the Magnolia State was both a "curse and a blessing." For white southerners who worked to address black immigrants' "dissatisfactions," see James R. Grossman, *Land of Hope: Chicago, Black Southerners, and the Great Migration* (Chicago: University of Chicago Press, 1989), 50.

8. Tuggle, *Another World Wonder*, 103.

9. Tuggle, *Another World Wonder*, 103.

10. Tuggle, *Another World Wonder*, 103.

11. Booker T. Washington, *Up from Slavery* (New York: Oxford University Press, 1995 [1901]), 23. Other African American Churches of Christ leaders gained inspiration from the words and works of Booker T. Washington. See Edward J. Robinson, *To*

Save My Race from Abuse: The Life of Samuel Robert Cassius (Tuscaloosa: University of Alabama Press, 2007); and Edward J. Robinson, *The Fight Is on in Texas: A History of African American Churches of Christ in the Lone Star State, 1865–2000* (Abilene, TX.: Abilene Christian University Press, 2008).

12. Tuggle, *Another World Wonder*, 104.

13. Tuggle, *Another World Wonder*, 104.

14. Linda O. McMurry, *George Washington Carver: Scientist and Symbol* (New York: Oxford University Press, 1981), 53, observes that "Washington ran his school like the 'master of a plantation,' but Carver refused to play the role of humble slave. The result was mutual respect for each other's abilities and aims, coupled with bitter clashes over policy and procedures. Carver's chosen 'mission field' proved to be considerably less than a paradise."

15. Tuggle, *Another World Wonder*, 108. As the next chapter will show, Tuggle often connected her personal experiences with poetry and scripture. Here she had in mind the Old Testament narrative in Genesis 22:7–8: "And Isaac spake unto Abraham his father, and said, My father: and he said, Here am I, my son. And he said, Behold the fire and the wood: but where is the lamb for a burnt offering? And Abraham said, My son, God will provide himself a lamb for a burnt offering: so they went both of them together."

16. Tuggle, *Another World Wonder*, 108. William Cullen Bryant (1794–1878) published the poem "Thanatopsis," a meditation on death in 1821. See Nina Baym et al., *The Norton Anthology of American Literature* (New York: W. W. Norton, 1989), 372–74.

17. Tuggle, *Another World Wonder*, 109.

18. In the first half of the twentieth century, the Brotherhood of Sleeping Car Porters, formed under the hegemony of A. Philip Randolph in 1925, consistently agitated for social justice and economic equality. See Jervis Anderson, *A. Philip Randolph: A Biographical Portrait* (New York: Harcourt Brace Jovanovich, 1972), 168; Paula F. Pfeffer, *A. Philip Randolph, Pioneer of the Civil Rights Movement* (Baton Rouge: Louisiana State University Press, 1990), 21–22; Eric Arnesen, *Brotherhoods of Color: Black Railroad Workers and the Struggle for Equality* (Cambridge, MA.: Harvard University Press, 2001), 84–85.

19. Tuggle, *Another World Wonder*, 110.

20. Tuggle, *Another World Wonder*, 110.

21. Tuggle, *Another World Wonder*, 111.

22. Anthea D. Butler, *Women in the Church of God in Christ: Making a Sanctified World* (Chapel Hill: University of North Carolina Press, 2007), 12. See also, Albert J. Raboteau, *Canaan Land: A Religious History of African Americans* (New York: Oxford University Press, 2001 [1999]), 47.

23. Tuggle, *Another World Wonder*, 112.

24. Tuggle, *Another World Wonder*, 60.

25. Annie C. Tuggle, *Our Ministers and Song Leaders of the Church of Christ* (Detroit, MI.: Annie C. Tuggle, 1945), 119. The Iowa and Lauderdale Church of Christ in Memphis, Tennessee, became the Vance Avenue Church of Christ in the 1950s, before

relocating and becoming the Norris Road Church of Christ in 1988. This information is in "Historical Sketch of the Norris Road Church of Christ" (in author's possession).

26. Tuggle, *Another World Wonder,* 112.

27. Tuggle, *Another World Wonder,* 113.

28. Tuggle, *Another World Wonder,* 113.

29. Alexander Campbell, "Work among the Colored People," *Gospel Advocate* 51 (December 2, 1909): 1523. The Union Avenue Church of Christ in Memphis, Tennessee, established in 1899, extended its beneficent hands to poor and oppressed people throughout its rich history. The Union Avenue members came to the rescue of victims of the 1937 flood. In the 1940s, they gave special assistance to Mary Carpenter, a young black widow and mother of three children. The congregation paid for her expenses through college as well as "for the care of her children while Mary was in school." See *The Story of a Church: Union Avenue Church of Christ* (n.p., n.d.), 14. The Union Avenue Church of Christ is now the Woodmont Hills Church of Christ in Cordova, Tennessee. Many thanks to Mary E. Rigney for sending the author this document. See also Nancy Craig Shelburne Codner, "A History of the Union Avenue Church of Christ, Memphis, Tennessee" (Masters thesis, Harding College Graduate School of Bible and Religion, 1960).

30. Tuggle, *Another World Wonder,* 115.

31. Tuggle, *Our Ministers and Song Leaders,* 119; Tuggle, *Another World Wonder,* 115.

32. Tuggle, *Another World Wonder,* 116.

33. Tuggle, *Another World Wonder,* 116.

34. Tuggle, *Another World Wonder,* 124. Tuggle, "The Bowser Christian Institute," *Christian Echo* 37 (August 5, 1942): 2.

35. Sara Harwell, "Nashville Christian Institute," in *The Encyclopedia of the Stone-Campbell Movement,* ed. Douglas A. Foster, Paul M. Blowers, Anthony L. Dunnavant, and D. Newell Williams (Grand Rapids, MI.: Eerdmans, 2004), 552.

36. Tuggle, *Another World Wonder,* 134.

37. Tuggle, *Another World Wonder,* 137. For a record of K. K. Mitchell's impressive ministerial career in Alabama, see Pearl Gray Daniels, *The History of the Holt Street Church of Christ and Its Role in Establishing Churches of Christ among African Americans in Central Alabama, 1928–1997* (Baltimore, MD.: American Literary Press, 1997), 67, 75–86, 264.

38. Tuggle, *Another World Wonder,* 138.

39. Interview with Fred D. Gray (May 8, 2009) at Pepperdine University, Malibu, California.

40. See Fred D. Gray, *Bus Ride to Justice, Changing the System by the System: The Life and Works of Fred D. Gray* (Montgomery, AL.: Black Belt Press, 1995).

41. Richard W. Thomas, "From Peasant to Proletarian: The Formation and Organization of the Black Industrial Working Class in Detroit, 1915–1945" (PhD dissertation, University of Michigan, 1976), 267, 305, 307, 310.

42. J. Randy Taraborrelli, *Diana Ross: An Unauthorized Biography* (New York: Citadel Press Books, 2007), 13.

43. Rosa Parks with Jim Haskins, *Rosa Parks: My Story* (New York: Dial Books, 1992), 161.

44. Berry Gordy, *To Be Loved: The Music, the Magic, the Memories of Motown: An Autobiography* (New York: Warner Books, 1994).

45. Tuggle, *Another World Wonder*, 147.

46. Tuggle, *Another World Wonder*, 151.

47. Milton C. Sernett, *Bound for the Promised Land: African-American Religion and the Great Migration* (Durham, N.C.: Duke University Press, 1997).

48. Willie David McClung, "Black Baptist Pastors, the Black Baptist Church, and Social Change: A Survey of Attitudes and Practices of Black Baptist Pastors from Selected Churches in Detroit" (PhD dissertation, Wayne State University, 1975), 63, 66, 67 (quote).

49. Darlene Clark Hine, *Hine Sight: Black Women and the Re-Construction of American History* (New York: Carlson Publishing, 1994), 131.

50. Richard W. Thomas, "The Black Urban Experience in Detroit: 1966–1967," in *Blacks and Chicanos in Urban Michigan*, ed. Homer C. Hawkins and Richard W. Thomas (Michigan Department of State: Michigan History Division, 1979), 79.

51. Tuggle, *Another World Wonder*, 154.

52. Tuggle, *Another World Wonder*, 156–57.

53. Tuggle, *Another World Wonder*, 171.

54. Tuggle, *Another World Wonder*, 173, 176 (Tuggle's quote).

55. Tuggle, *Another World Wonder*, 176.

56. Tuggle, *Another World Wonder*, 171.

57. Tuggle, *Another World Wonder*, 172.

Chapter 5

1. Annie C. Tuggle, *Another World Wonder* (n.p., n.d.), 6. For the story of Hannah, see 1 Samuel 1:1–28.

2. Tuggle, *Another World Wonder*, 22.

3. Albert J. Raboteau, *Slave Religion: The "Invisible Institution" in the Antebellum South* (New York: Oxford University Press, 1978), 238–43; John W. Blassingame, *The Slave Community: Plantation Life in the Antebellum South* (New York: Oxford University Press, 1979 [1972]), 130, 133. Allen Dwight Callahan, *The Talking Book: African Americans and the Bible* (New Haven, CT.: Yale University, 2006), 20, observes that "African Americans were learning en masse to read the Bible as a book opened and closed. As the Word of God, it spoke to them with words that lent a new language to their dreams and their nightmares. As a written text, it greeted them with silence. But as they struggled to make the book talk to them, African Americans would make the Talking Book their own."

4. Vincent L. Wimbush, "The Bible and African Americans: An Outline of an Interpretive History," in *Stony the Road We Trod: African American Biblical Interpretation*, ed. Cain Hope Felder (Minneapolis: Fortress, 1991), 94.

5. Wimbush, "The Bible and African Americans," 96.

6. Tuggle, *Another World Wonder*, 11–12. Here Tuggle's commitment to reading the Bible is strikingly similar to Maria W. Stewart (1803–1879), a black female reformer from Boston who denounced the institution of chattel enslavement. Stewart asserted that "I have borrowed much of my language from the Holy Bible. During childhood and youth, it was the book that I mostly studied and now, while my hands are toiling for their daily sustenance, my heart is most generally mediating upon its divine truth." Maria W. Stewart, *Productions of Mrs. Maria Stewart* (Boston: Friends of Freedom and Virtue, 1835), 11; Delores C. Carpenter, "Black Women in Religious Institutions: A Historical Summary from Slavery to the 1960s," in *Down by the Riverside: Readings in African American Religion*, ed. Larry G. Murphy (New York: New York University Press, 2000), 98.

7. Tuggle, *Another World Wonder*, 109.

8. Tuggle, *Another World Wonder*, 198.

9. Tuggle, *Another World Wonder*, 198.

10. Charles Marsh, *God's Long Summer: Stories of Faith and Civil Rights* (Princeton, N.J.: Princeton University Press, 1997), 22–23; Cheryl J. Sanders, "African Americans, the Bible, and Spiritual Formation," in *African Americans and the Bible: Sacred Texts and Social Textures*, ed. Vincent L. Wimbush (New York: Continuum, 2000), 599.

11. Richard T. Hughes, *Reviving the Ancient Faith: The Story of Churches of Christ* (Grand Rapids, MI.: Eerdmans, 1996), 50, asserts that baptism for the remission of sins is "a theme that would become a central plank in the doctrinal structure of Churches of Christ." See also David W. Fletcher, ed., *Baptism and the Remission of Sins: An Historical Perspective* (Joplin, MO.: College Press, 1990).

12. Tuggle, *Another World Wonder*, 10.

13. Edward J. Robinson, *Show Us How You Do It: Marshall Keeble and the Rise of Black Churches of Christ in the United States, 1914–1968* (Tuscaloosa: University of Alabama Press, 2008), 47–55.

14. M. Eugene Boring, *Disciples and the Bible: A History of Disciples Biblical Interpretation in North America* (St. Louis, MO.: Chalice Press, 1997), 277–79; quote on 277.

15. Tuggle, *Another World Wonder*, 201.

16. David H. Warren, "Nicholas Broadie Hardeman," in *Encyclopedia of the Stone-Campbell Movement*, ed. Douglas A. Foster, Anthony L. Dunnavant, Paul M. Blowers, and Newell D. Williams (Grand Rapids, MI.: Eerdmans, 2004), 381; Hughes, *Reviving the Ancient Faith*, 199; Leroy Garrett, *The Stone-Campbell Movement: An Anecdotal History of Three Churches* (Joplin, MO.: College Press, 1981), 684–85.

17. N. B. Hardeman, *Hardeman's Tabernacle Sermons* (Nashville, TN.: McQuiddy Printing Company, 1923), 241, 245.

18. Annie C. Tuggle, "Among the Colored Folks," *Gospel Advocate* 64 (August 31, 1922): 837.

19. Annie C. Tuggle, "The Hardeman-Smith Meeting," *Gospel Advocate* 65 (May 3, 1923): 445.

20. Tuggle, *Another World Wonder*, 13.

21. Tuggle, *Another World Wonder*, 14. Other black leaders in Churches of Christ similarly espoused an exclusivistic posture and argued that they were right while all other religious groups were wrong. Edward J. Robinson, *To Save My Race from Abuse: The Life of Samuel Robert Cassius* (Tuscaloosa: University of Alabama Press, 2007), 164, notes that Cassius preached to demonstrate to Baptists, Methodists, Catholics, Pentecostals, and all other denominations that "I am right and they are wrong."

22. Tuggle, *Another World Wonder*, 14–15.

23. In this regard, Tuggle held the same theological position of such white leaders as David Lipscomb, who believed in the complete equality of women, but "his legalistic understanding of the Bible" meant that females could not assume leadership roles in the church. See Boring, *Disciples and the Bible*, 277. See also Forrest G. Wood, *The Arrogance of Faith: Christianity and Race in America from the Colonial Era to the Twentieth Century* (New York: Alfred A. Knopf, 1990). Wood's thorough work treats primarily the haughty attitudes and racial hubris of white Christians toward African Americans during the eras of chattel enslavement and de jure segregation, yet his scholarly assessment also applies to Tuggle and other members of African American Churches of Christ who have historically exhibited attitudes of religious superiority toward their black neighbors.

24. Tuggle, *Another World Wonder*, 15–16.

25. Tuggle, *Another World Wonder*, 29.

26. Tuggle, *Another World Wonder*, 32. Tuggle's quotation comes from Romans 8:28.

27. Tuggle, *Another World Wonder*, 40.

28. Members of the Churches of Christ viewed themselves as "New Testament Christians" and regarded the New Testament as more authoritative than the Old Testament.

29. Tuggle, *Another World Wonder*, 60.

30. Tuggle, *Another World Wonder*, 60–61. The verses Tuggle pieced together were 2 Kings 6:15–17 and 1 Corinthians 2:2.

31. Tuggle, *Another World Wonder*, 62. The story of Jacob's dream appears in Genesis 28:12 and John 1:51.

32. Tuggle, *Another World Wonder*, 62.

33. Tuggle, *Another World Wonder*, 43.

34. Tuggle, *Another World Wonder*, 134.

35. Jarena Lee, "Religious Experience and Journal of Mrs. Jarena Lee" [1849], in *My Soul Has Grown Deep: Classics of Early African-American Literature*, ed. John Edgar Wideman (Philadelphia: Running Press, 2001), 87. In this quote, Lee combined biblical references from Daniel 5:1–9 and Luke 18:13.

36. Tuggle, *Another World Wonder*, 46.

37. Tuggle, *Another World Wonder*, 47. In the spring of 1914, an ailing David Lipscomb was eighty-three and wheelchair bound. See Robert Hooper, *Crying in the Wilderness: A Biography of David Lipscomb* (Nashville, TN.: David Lipscomb College, 1979), 316, 318.

38. Tuggle, *Another World Wonder,* 47. Tuggle's commendation of the Lipscomb couple corroborates the observation of historian Robert Hooper that "Their concern for others overrode their own interests." Hooper, *Crying in the Wilderness,* 318.

39. Tuggle, *Another World Wonder,* 47, 78.

40. Tuggle, *Another World Wonder,* 115.

41. Tuggle, *Another World Wonder,* 138.

42. Tuggle, *Another World Wonder,* 80.

Chapter 6

1. Exemplary of African American women who shared their story of God's working in their lives are: Jarena Lee, *Religious Experience and Journal of Mrs. Jarena Lee* [1849], in *My Soul Has Grown Deep: Classics of Early African-American Literature,* ed. John Edgar Wideman (Philadelphia: Running Press, 2001), 79–186; Sojourner Truth, *Narrative of Sojourner Truth* (New York: Penguin Books, 1998 [1850]); Harriet A. Jacobs, *Incidents in the Life of a Slave Girl, Written by Herself* (Cambridge, MA.: Harvard University Press, 1987 [1861]); Alfreda M. Duster, ed., *Crusade for Justice: The Autobiography of Ida B. Wells* (Chicago: University of Chicago Press, 1970); Mary Church Terrell, *A Colored Woman in a White World* (Washington, D.C.: National Association of Colored Women's Club Inc., 1968 [1940]); and Anne Moody, *Coming of Age in Mississippi* (New York: Laurel, 1968). See also William L. Andrews, *To Tell a Free Story: The First Century of Afro-American Autobiography, 1760–1865* (Urbana: University of Illinois Press, 1986); William L. Andrews, ed., *Sisters of the Spirit: Three Black Women's Autobiographies of the Nineteenth Century* (Bloomington: Indiana University Press, 1986). For the statistical information for African Americans in California, see Quintard Taylor, *In Search of the Racial Frontier: African Americans in the American West, 1528–1990* (New York: W. W. Norton, 1998), 279.

2. Terrell, introduction to *A Colored Woman in a White World.*

3. Annie C. Tuggle, acknowledgement to *Another World Wonder* (n.p., n.d.). Unlike many contemporary white and black members of Churches of Christ who repudiated any affiliation and connection to previous religious leaders, Tuggle, for the most part, refused to ignore or deny her historical "roots." See C. Leonard Allen and Richard T. Hughes, *Discovering Our Roots: The Ancestry of Churches of Christ* (Abilene, TX.: Abilene Christian University Press, 1988).

4. Tuggle, introduction to *Another World Wonder.*

5. Tuggle, preface to *Another World Wonder.*

6. Tuggle, *Another World Wonder,* 20.

7. Tuggle, *Another World Wonder,* 35–36. G. P. Hamilton was one of the influential black men in the first few decades of the twentieth century. See G. P. Hamilton, *The Bright Side of Memphis* (Memphis, TN.: Burke's Book Store, 1908).

8. Tuggle, *Another World Wonder,* 94–95.

9. Tuggle, *Another World Wonder,* 142.

10. Tuggle, *Another World Wonder,* 165.

11. Tuggle, *Another World Wonder,* 185.

12. Tuggle, *Another World Wonder*, 186.

13. Tuggle, *Another World Wonder*, 218.

14. Tuggle, preface to *Another World Wonder*.

15. For Tuggle's discussion of her family, see *Another World Wonder*, 1–6. The quote is from Martin Luther King Jr., *Strength to Love* (Philadelphia: Fortress, 1981 [1963]), 42. See also Douglas A. Blackmon, *Slavery by Another Name: The Re-Enslavement of Black Americans from the Civil War to World War II* (New York: Anchor Books, 2009).

16. Tuggle, *Another World Wonder*, 201.

17. Marshall Keeble, "Keeble to be Here," *Gospel Advocate* 83 (December 25, 1941): 1,242.

18. Tuggle, *Another World Wonder*, 54–55.

19. Tuggle, *Another World Wonder*, 64. See Edward J. Robinson, *The Fight Is on in Texas: A History of African American Churches of Christ in the Lone Star State, 1865–2000* (Abilene, TX.: Abilene Christian University Press, 2008), 119–34.

20. Tuggle, *Another World Wonder*, 84–85. See also Robinson, *Show Us How You Do It*, 121–22.

21. Tuggle, *Another World Wonder*, 137–38.

22. Tuggle, *Another World Wonder*, 167.

23. James R. Grossman, *"Land of Hope": Chicago, Black Southerners, and the Great Migration* (Chicago: University of Chicago Press, 1989).

24. Tuggle, *Another World Wonder*, 17.

25. Tuggle, *Another World Wonder*, 29.

26. Tuggle, *Another World Wonder*, 23–24.

27. Tuggle, *Another World Wonder*, 21.

28. Tuggle, *Another World Wonder*, 36.

29. Tuggle, *Another World Wonder*, 89–90.

30. Tuggle, *Another World Wonder*, 104, 111.

31. Tuggle, *Another World Wonder*, 110.

32. Tuggle, *Another World Wonder*, 48.

33. Tuggle, *Another World Wonder*, 55.

34. Tuggle, *Another World Wonder*, 64.

35. Tuggle, *Another World Wonder*, 58.

36. Tuggle, *Another World Wonder*, 69.

37. Tuggle, *Another World Wonder*, 87.

38. Tuggle, *Another World Wonder*, 85.

39. In this regard, Tuggle held the same view as Marshall Keeble, who, after he baptized more than one thousand people in 1931, testified that "The white churches sponsored all of this work." Keeble, "Sowing and Reaping," *Gospel Advocate* 74 (January 28, 1932): 124. See also Robinson, *Show Us How You Do It*, 73–98.

40. Tuggle, *Another World Wonder*, 104.

41. Tuggle, *Another World Wonder*, 68.

42. Tuggle, *Another World Wonder*, 119–22.

43. Tuggle, *Another World Wonder*, 36, 41.

44. Tuggle, *Another World Wonder*, 25. See also Edgar Allan Poe, "The Raven," in *The Norton Anthology of American Literature*, Nina Baym et al. (New York: W. W. Norton, 1989): 596.

45. Tuggle, *Another World Wonder*, 28.

46. Tuggle, *Another World Wonder*, 32–34.

47. Tuggle, *Another World Wonder*, 81–82.

48. Tuggle, *Another World Wonder*, 120.

49. Tuggle, *Another World Wonder*, 148.

50. Tuggle, *Another World Wonder*, 78.

51. Tuggle, *Another World Wonder*, 201.

52. Tuggle, *Another World Wonder*, 201.

53. Annie C. Tuggle, "Getting the Most out of Life," *Gospel Advocate* 64 (November 9, 1922): 1,075. Here Tuggle refers to Plato's quote from *The Republic*, VIII, in *Plato: Apology, Crito, Phaedo, Symposium, Republic*, ed. B. Jowett (Roslyn, N.Y.: Walter J. Black, 1969 [1942]), 451.

54. Tuggle, *Another World Wonder*, 79.

Epilogue

1. Annie C. Tuggle, *Another World Wonder* (n.p., n.d.), 53.
2. Tuggle, *Another World Wonder*, 116.
3. Tuggle, *Another World Wonder*, 134.
4. Tuggle, *Another World Wonder*, 61.

SELECTED BIBLIOGRAPHY

Newspapers

Christian Echo (Fort Smith, Arkansas), 1942.
Christian Leader (Cincinnati, Ohio), 1922.
Christian Leader and the Way (Cincinnati, Ohio), 1907.
Christian Standard (Cincinnati, Ohio), 1868, 1880.
Daily Memphis Enquirer (Memphis, Tennessee), 1848.
Gospel Advocate (Nashville, Tennessee), 1915, 1916, 1921–1923, 1932, 1937, 1939, 1968.
Leaven (Malibu, California), 1995.
Memphis Daily Appeal (Memphis, Tennessee), 1855, 1857.

Government Sources

1850 United States Federal Census: Slave Schedules. Shelby County, Tennessee.
1860 United States Federal Census. Shelby County, Tennessee.
Rowland, Helen. *Shelby County, Tennessee Newspaper Abstracts through 1859*. Signal Mountain, TN.: Mountain Press, 2002.

Primary Sources

Andrews, William L., ed. *Sisters of the Spirit: Three Black Women's Autobiographies of the Nineteenth Century*. Bloomington: Indiana University Press, 1986.
Baker, Ray Stannard. *Following the Color Line: American Negro Citizenship in the Progressive Era*. New York: Harper & Row, 1964 [1908].
Barnard, Hollinger F., ed. *Outside the Magic Circle: The Autobiography of Virginia Foster Durr*. Tuscaloosa: University of Alabama Press, 1986.
Baym, Nina, et al. *The Norton Anthology of American Literature*. New York: W. W. Norton, 1989.
Douglass, Frederick. *My Bondage and My Freedom*. New York: Dover, 1969 [1855].
Douglass, Frederick. *Narrative of the Life of Frederick Douglass, An American Slave*. New York: Penguin Books, 1986 [1845].
Duster, Alfreda M., ed. *Crusade for Justice: The Autobiography of Ida B. Wells*. Chicago: University of Chicago Press, 1970.

Gray, Fred D. *Bus Ride to Justice, Changing the System by the System: The Life and Works of Fred D. Gray*. Montgomery, AL.: Black Belt Press, 1995.

Hardeman, N. B. *Hardeman's Tabernacle Sermons*. Nashville: McQuiddy Printing, 1923.

Holland, Endesha Ida Mae. *From the Mississippi Delta: A Memoir*. Chicago: Lawrence Hill Brooks, 1997.

Jacobs, Harriet A. *Incidents in the Life of a Slave Girl, Written by Herself*. Cambridge, MA.: Harvard University Press, 1987 [1861].

Jowett, B., editor. *Plato: Apology, Crito, Phaedo, Symposium, Republic*. Roslyn, N.Y.: Walter J. Black, 1969 [1942].

Kipling, Rudyard. *Rudyard Kipling's Verse*. New York: Doubleday, Doran, 1945.

Laney, Lucy Craft. "The Burden of the Educated Colored Woman." *Report of the Hampton Negro Conference*. July 1899.

Lerner, Gerda, ed. *Black Women in White America: A Documentary History*. New York: Vintage Books, 1972.

Lewis, David Levering, ed. *W. E. B. Du Bois: A Reader*. New York: Henry Holt, 1995.

Mays, Benjamin E. *Born to Rebel: An Autobiography*. New York: Charles Scribner's Sons, 1971.

Moody, Anne. *Coming of Age in Mississippi*. New York: Laurel Book, 1968.

Murphy, Larry G., ed. *Down by the Riverside: Readings in African American Religion*. New York: New York University Press, 2000.

Northup, Solomon. *Twelve Years a Slave*. Mineola, N.Y.: Dover, 1970 [1853].

Parks, Rosa, with James Haskins. *Rosa Parks: My Story*. New York: Dial Books, 1992.

Riggs, Marcia Y. *Can I Get a Witness?: Prophetic Religious Voices of African American Women: An Anthology*. New York: Orbis Books, 1997.

Sterling, Dorothy, ed. *We Are Your Sisters: Black Women in the Nineteenth Century*. New York: W. W. Norton, 1997 [1984].

Stewart, Maria W. *Productions of Mrs. Maria Stewart*. Boston: Friends of Freedom and Virtue, 1835.

Terrell, Mary Church. *A Colored Woman in a White World*. Washington, D.C.: National Association of Colored Women's Club Inc., 1968 [1940].

Truth, Sojourner. *Narrative of Sojourner Truth*. New York: Penguin Books, 1998 [1850].

Tuggle, Annie. C. *Another World Wonder*. n.p., n.d.

Washington, Booker T. *Up from Slavery*. New York: Oxford University Press, 1995 [1901].

Wideman, John Edgar, ed. *My Soul Has Grown Deep: Classics of Early African- American Literature*. Philadelphia: Running Press, 2001.

Secondary Sources

Allen, C. Leonard, and Richard T. Hughes. *Discovering Our Roots: The Ancestry of Churches of Christ.* Abilene, TX.: Abilene Christian University Press, 1988.

Anderson, Jervis. *A Philip Randolph: A Biographical Portrait.* New York: Harcourt Brace Jovanovich, 1972.

Arnesen, Eric. *Brotherhoods of Color: Black Railroad Workers and the Struggle for Equality.* Cambridge, MA.: Harvard University Press, 2001.

Baldwin, Lewis V. *"Invisible" Strands in African Methodism: A History of the African Union Methodist and American Methodist Episcopal Churches, 1805–1980.* Metuchen, N.J.: Scarecrow, 1983.

Banner, Lois W. *Women in Modern America: A Brief History.* San Diego: Harcourt Brace Jovanovich, 1984 [1974].

Bass, Jack, and W. Scott Poole. *The Palmetto State: The Making of Modern South Carolina.* Columbia: University of South Carolina Press, 2009.

Berry, Mary Frances, and John W. Blassingame. *Long Memory: The Black Experience in America.* New York: Oxford University Press, 1982.

Blackmon, Douglas A. *Slavery by Another Name: The Re-Enslavement of Black American from the Civil War to World War II.* New York: Anchor Books, 2009.

Blassingame, John W. *The Slave Community: Plantation Life in the Antebellum South.* New York: Oxford University Press, 1979 [1972].

Bodenhorn, Howard. "The Mulatto Advantage: The Biological Consequences in Rural Antebellum Virginia." *Journal of Interdisciplinary History* 33 (Summer 2002): 21–46.

Boring, M. Eugene. *Disciples and the Bible: A History of Disciples Biblical Interpretation in North America.* St. Louis, MO.: Chalice Press, 1997.

Bowers, Calvin H. *Realizing the California Dream: The Story of the Black Churches of Christ in Los Angeles.* Calvin H. Bowers, 2001.

Boyd, R. Vernon. *Undying Dedication: The Story of G. P. Bowser.* Nashville, TN.: Gospel Advocate Company, 1985.

Brown, Teresa L. Fry. *God Don't Like Ugly: African American Women Handing on Spiritual Values.* Nashville, TN.: Abingdon, 2000.

Butler, Anthea D. *Women in the Church of God in Christ: Making a Sanctified World.* Chapel Hill: University of North Carolina Press, 2007.

Callahan, Allen Dwight. *The Talking Book: African Americans and the Bible.* New Haven, CT.: Yale University Press, 2006.

Chesler, Ellen. *Woman of Valor: Margaret Sanger and the Birth Control Movement In America.* New York: Simon & Schuster, 1992.

Choate, J. E. *Roll Jordan Roll: A Biography of Marshall Keeble.* Nashville, TN.: Gospel Advocate Company, 1974.

Connelly, Mark Thomas. *The Response to Prostitution in the Progressive Era*. Chapel Hill: University of North Carolina Press, 1980.

Connelly, Matthew. *Fatal Misconception: The Struggle to Control World Population*. Cambridge, MA.: Harvard University Press, 2008.

Daniels, Pearl Gray. *The History of the Holt Street Church of Christ and Its Role in Establishing Churches of Christ among African Americans in Central Alabama, 1928–1997*. Baltimore, MD.: American Literary Press, 1997.

Dray, Philip. *At the Hands of Persons Unknown: The Lynching of Black America*. New York: The Modern Library, 2003.

Evans, Curtis J. *The Burden of Black Religion*. New York: Oxford University Press, 2008.

Felder, Cain Hope, ed. *Stony the Road We Trod: African American Biblical Interpretation*. Minneapolis: Fortress, 1991.

Fields, Barbara Jeanne. *Slavery and Freedom on the Middle Ground: Maryland during the Nineteenth Century*. New Haven, CT.: Yale University Press, 1985.

Fleming, Cynthia Griggs. *Soon We Will Not Cry: The Liberation of Ruby Doris Smith Robinson*. Lanham, MD.: Rowman & Littlefield, 1998.

Fletcher, David W., ed. *Baptism and the Remission of Sins: An Historical Perspective*. Joplin, MO.: College Press Publishing, 1990.

Foster, Douglas A., Paul M. Blowers, Anthony L. Dunnavant, and D. Newell Williams. *The Encyclopedia of the Stone-Campbell Movement*. Grand Rapids, MI.: Eerdmans, 2004.

Garrett, Leroy. *The Stone-Campbell Movement: An Anecdotal History of Three Churches*. Joplin, MO.: College Press, 1981.

Gatewood, Willard B. *Aristocrats of Color: The Black Elite, 1880–1920*. Bloomington: Indiana University Press, 1990.

Giddings, Paula J. *Ida, A Sword among Lions: Ida B. Wells and the Campaign against Lynching*. New York: Amistad, 2008.

Giddings, Paula J. *When and Where I Enter: The Impact of Black Women on Race and Sex in America*. New York: William Morrow, 1984.

Gilkes, Cheryl. *If It Wasn't for the Women: Black Women's Experience and Womanist Culture in Church and Community*. Maryknoll, N.Y.: Orbis Books, 2001.

Goodpasture, B. C. *Marshall Keeble: Biography and Sermons*. Nashville, TN.: Gospel Advocate Company, 1966 [1931].

Gordy, Berry. *To Be Loved: The Music, the Magic, the Memories of Motown: An Autobiography*. New York: Warner Books, 1994.

Grossman, James R. *Land of Hope: Chicago, Black Southerners, and the Great Migration*. Chicago: University of Chicago Press, 1989.

Gutman, Herbert G. *The Black Family in Slavery and Freedom, 1750–1925.* New York: Vintage Books, 1976.

Hale, Grace Elizabeth. *Making Whiteness: The Culture of Segregation in the South, 1890-1940.* New York: Pantheon Books, 1998.

Hamilton, G. P. *The Bright Side of Memphis.* Memphis, TN.: Burke's Book Store, 1908.

Harrell, David Edwin. *Sources of Division in the Disciples of Christ, 1865–1900: A Social History of the Disciples of Christ.* Tuscaloosa: University of Alabama Press, 2003 [1973].

Hatch, Nathan O. *The Democratization of American Christianity.* New Haven, CT.: Yale University Press, 1989.

Higginbotham, Evelyn Brooks. *Righteous Discontent: The Women's Movement in the Black Baptist Church, 1880–1920.* Cambridge, MA.: Harvard University Press, 1993.

Hine, Darlene Clark, and Kathleen Thompson. *A Shining Thread of Hope: The History of Black Women in America.* New York: Broadway Books, 1998.

Hine, Darlene Clark. *Hine Sight: Black Women and the Re-Construction of American History.* New York: Carlson Publishing, 1994.

Hooper, Robert. *A Distinct People: A History of the Churches of Christ in the 20th Century.* West Monroe, LA.: Howard Publishing, 1993.

Hooper, Robert. *Crying in the Wilderness: A Biography of David Lipscomb.* Nashville, TN.: David Lipscomb College, 1979.

Hughes, Richard T. *Reviving the Ancient Faith: The Story of Churches of Christ in America.* Grand Rapids, MI.: Eerdmans, 1996.

Hughes, Richard T., and R. L. Roberts. *The Churches of Christ.* Westport, CT.: Greenwood, 2001.

Hutchins, Fred L. *What Happened in Memphis.* Kingsport, TN.: Kingspor, 1965.

Johnson, James Weldon. *The Autobiography of an Ex-Colored Man.* New York: Penguin Books, 1990 [1912].

Johnson, Katie N. *Sisters in Sin: Brothel Drama in America, 1900–1920.* New York: Cambridge University Press, 2006.

Jones, Jacqueline. *Labor of Love, Labor of Sorrow: Black Women, Work, and the Family, from Slavery to the Present.* New York: Vintage Books, 1986.

King Jr., Martin Luther. *Strength to Love.* Philadelphia: Fortress, 1981 [1963].

Kolchin, Peter. *American Slavery, 1619–1877.* New York: Hill and Wang, 1993.

Lamon, Lester C. *Black Tennesseans, 1900–1930.* Knoxville: University of Tennessee Press, 1977.

Lee, Chana Kai. *For Freedom's Sake: The Life of Fannie Lou Hamer*. Urbana: University of Illinois Press, 1999.

Levine, Lawrence W. *Black Culture and Black Consciousness: Afro-American Folk Thought from Slavery to Freedom*. New York: Oxford University Press, 1978.

Marsh, Charles. *God's Long Summer: Stories of Faith and Civil Rights*. Princeton, N.J.: Princeton University Press, 1997.

McMillen, Neil R. *Dark Journey: Black Mississippians in the Age of Jim Crow*. Urbana: University of Illinois Press, 1990.

McMurry, Linda O. *George Washington Carver: Scientist and Symbol*. New York: Oxford University Press, 1981.

McMurry, Linda O. *To Keep the Waters Troubled: The Life of Ida B. Wells*. New York: Oxford University Press, 1998.

Murch, James DeForest. *Christians Only: A History of the Restoration Movement*. Cincinnati, OH.: Standard Publishing, 1962.

Neverdon-Morton, Cynthia. *Afro-American Women of the South and the Advancement of the Race, 1895–1925*. Knoxville: University of Tennessee Press, 1989.

Newman, Richard S. *Freedom's Prophet: Bishop Richard Allen, the AME Church And the Black Founding Fathers*. New York: New York University Press, 2008.

Oakes, James. *The Ruling Race: A History of American Slaveholders*. New York: Knopf, 1982.

Odem, Mary E. *Delinquent Daughters: Protecting and Policing Adolescent Female Sexuality in the United States, 1885–1920*. Chapel Hill: University of North Carolina Press, 1996.

Painter, Nell Irvin. *Standing at Armageddon: The United States, 1877–1919*. New York: W. W. Norton, 1987.

Pfeffer, Paula F. *A. Philip Randolph, Pioneer of the Civil Rights Movement*. Baton Rouge: Louisiana State University Press, 1990.

Phillips, C. H. *The History of the Colored Methodist Episcopal Church in America*. New York: Arno, 1972.

Raboteau, Albert J. *Canaan Land: A Religious History of African Americans*. New York: Oxford University Press, 2001 [1999].

Raboteau, Albert J. *Slave Religion: The "Invisible Institution" in the Antebellum South*. New York: Oxford University Press, 1978.

Robinson, Edward J. *Show Us How You Do It: Marshall Keeble and the Rise of Black Churches of Christ, 1914–1968*. Tuscaloosa: University of Alabama Press, 2008.

Robinson, Edward J. *The Fight Is on in Texas: A History of African American Churches of Christ in the Lone Star State, 1865–2000*. Abilene, TX.: Abilene Christian University Press, 2008.

Robinson, Edward J. *To Save My Race from Abuse: The Life of Samuel Robert Cassius*. Tuscaloosa: University of Alabama Press, 2007.

Rochester, Anna. *The Populist Movement in the United States*. New York: International Publishers, 1943.

Rosen, Ruth. *The Lost Sisterhood: Prostitution in America, 1900–1918*. Baltimore, MD.: Johns Hopkins University Press, 1982.

Rothman, Joshua D. *Notorious in the Neighborhood: Sex and Family across the Color Line in Virginia, 1787–1861*. Chapel Hill: University of North Carolina Press, 2003.

Russell, Kathy, Midge Wilson, and Ronald Hall. *The Color Complex: The Politics of Skin Color among African Americans*. New York: Harcourt Brace Jovanovich, 1992.

Savage, Horace C. *Life and Times of Bishop Isaac Lane*. Nashville, TN.: National Publication Company, 1958.

Schweninger, Loren. *Black Property Owners in the South, 1790–1915*. Urbana: University of Illinois Press, 1990.

Sernett, Milton C. *Bound for the Promised Land: African-American Religion and the Great Migration*. Durham, N.C.: Duke University Press, 1997.

Sigafoos, Robert A. *Cotton Row to Beale Street: A Business History of Memphis*. Memphis, TN.: Memphis State University Press, 1979.

Shlaes, Amity. *The Forgotten Man: A New History of the Great Depression*. New York: HarperCollins, 2007.

Stammp, Kenneth M. *The Peculiar Institution: Slavery in the Antebellum South*. New York: Vintage Books, 1956.

Summers, Mark W. *The Gilded Age, or the Hazard of New Functions*. Upper Saddle River, N.J.: Prentice, 1997.

Taraborrelli, J. Randy. *Diana Ross: An Unauthorized Biography*. New York: Citadel Press Books, 2007.

Taylor, Quintard. *In Search of the Racial Frontier: African Americans in the American West, 1528–1990*. New York: W. W. Norton, 1998.

Thirty Years of Lynching in the United States, 1889–1918. New York: Arno, 1969.

Troeltsch, Ernst. *The Social Teaching of the Christian Churches*. Volume 1. New York: MacMillan, 1950 [1931].

Walker, Alice. *In Search of Our Mothers' Gardens*. San Diego: Harcourt Brace Jovanovich, 1983 [1967].

West, Earl. *The Life and Times of David Lipscomb*. Germantown, TN.: Religious Book Service, 1987.

White, Deborah Gray. *Ar'n't I a Woman?: Female Slaves in the Plantation South*. New York: W. W. Norton, 1985.

White, Deborah Gray. *Too Heavy a Load: Black Women in Defense of Themselves,1894-1994.* New York: W. W. Norton, 1999.

Wimbush, Vincent L., ed. *African Americans and the Bible: Sacred Texts and Social Textures*. New York: Continuum, 2000.

Wood, Forrest G. *The Arrogance of Faith: Christianity and Race in America from the Colonial Era to the Twentieth Century*. New York: Alfred A. Knopf, 1990.

Woodward, C. Vann. *Origins of the New South*. Baton Rouge: Louisiana State University Press, 1997 [1951].

Wynkoop, Mildred Bangs. *The Trevecca Story: 75 Years of Christian Service.* Nashville, TN.: Trevecca, 1976.

Unpublished Materials

Berkeley, Kathleen Christine. "'Like A Plague of Locust': Immigration and Social Change in Memphis, Tennessee, 1850–1880." PhD dissertation, University of California, Los Angeles, 1980.

Bond, Beverly Greene. "'Till Fair Aurora Rise': African American Women in Memphis, Tennessee, 1840–1915." PhD dissertation, University of Memphis, 1996.

Bunch-Lyons, Beverly A. "And They Came: The Migration of African-American Women from the South to Cincinnati, Ohio, 1900–1950." PhD dissertation, Miami University, 1995.

Codner, Nancy Craig Shelburne. "A History of the Union Avenue Church of Christ, Memphis, Tennessee." Masters thesis, Harding College Graduate School of Bible and Religion, 1960.

Cottingham, Britt Edward. "The Burden of the Educated Woman: Lucy Laney and Haines Institute, 1886–1933." Masters thesis, Georgia State University, 1995.

Edwards, Ishmell Hendrex. "A History of Rust College." PhD dissertation, University of Mississippi, 1993.

Jackson, Alicia K. "The Colored Methodist Episcopal Church and Their Struggle for Autonomy and Reform in the New South." PhD dissertation, University of Mississippi, 2004.

Giffin, William Wayne. "The Negro in Ohio, 1914–1939." PhD dissertation, Ohio State University, 1968.

Griffin, Paul R. "Black Founders of Reconstruction Era Methodist Colleges: Daniel A. Payne, Joseph C. Price, and Isaac Lane, 1863–1890." PhD dissertation, Emory University, 1983.

Kornbluh, Andrea Tuttle. "'The Bowl of Promise': Cincinnati Social Welfare Planners, Cultural Pluralism and the Metropolitan Community, 1911–1952. PhD dissertation, University of Cincinnati, 1988.

McClung, Willie David. "Black Baptist Pastors, The Black Baptist Church and Social Change: A Survey of Attitudes and Practices of Black Detroit

Pastors from Selected Churches in Detroit." PhD dissertation, Wayne State University, 1975.

Melton, Gloria Brown. "Blacks in Memphis, Tennessee, 1920–1955: A Historical Study." PhD dissertation, Washington State University, 1982.

Phillips, C. Myer. "A Historical Study of the Attitude of the Churches of Christ Toward Other Denominations." PhD dissertation, Baylor University, 1983.

The Story of a Church: Union Avenue Church of Christ. N.p., n.d.

Thomas, Richard Walter. "From Peasant to Proletarian: The Formation and Organization of the Black Industrial Working Class in Detroit, 1915–1945." PhD dissertation, University of Michigan, 1976.

INDEX